YOUTH MINISTRY AND EVANGELISM
New Wine for a New Day

Shirley F. Clement
Thomas L. Salsgiver

DISCIPLESHIP RESOURCES
MATERIALS FOR GROWTH IN CHRISTIAN FAITH AND LIFE
P.O. Box 189 • Nashville, TN 37202 • Phone (615) 340-7284

Reprinted 1992.

ISBN 0-88177-094-9

Library of Congress Card Catalog No. 90-83150

All scripture quotations unless otherwise noted are from the New Revised Standard Version, 1990.

DR094B

DEDICATION

To Joanne, a constant, steady, and loving support; to Becky, Brent, and Renee, young people who enrich and give meaning to our lives.

CONTENTS

INTRODUCTION

A re you an adult concerned about youth ministry and evangelism? Are you a volunteer in your church's youth ministry, a paid youth worker, a Christian educator, a diaconal minister, a youth minister, a pastor? If you are, this book is for you.

The General Board of Discipleship of The United Methodist Church has developed an agenda for youth ministry. This statement focuses on the primary tasks of those involved in youth ministry: to love youth where they are, to encourage them in developing their relationship with God, to provide them with opportunities for nurture and growth, and to challenge them to respond to God's call to serve in their communities. Our aim in this book is to expand upon this statement as it relates to youth evangelism.

We will begin by providing a biblical foundation for looking at evangelism with youth. The biblical image of wine and wineskins (Mark 2:22) lays a foundation for our discussion. Jesus taught that life and power of his Spirit (new wine) cannot be contained by old forms of ministry (old wineskins).

With this biblical foundation in mind, we will look at the youth of the '90s. We believe that any attempt to explore youth evangelism must take into account who youth are in the '90s. What forms of ministry are needed today to address issues such as sexual practice, drug use, physical abuse, self-esteem, and home/family dysfunction? What stereotypes and "myth-conceptions" do we have—about adults, about youth, and about evangelism—that need to be broken down in order for us to enter more effectively into ministry?

Our ultimate objective is to think more creatively about what Jesus meant when he recommended "new wineskins." What would it look like to create ministries with youth in which the radical nature of the gospel has indeed transformed lives and challenged youth to reach out to others? We will share some examples where this has occurred. Our hope is to provide a springboard for adult leaders with youth to create their own models of youth ministry and evangelism appropriate to their own context.

CHAPTER 1
SETTING THE FRAMEWORK

Welcome to the world of youth ministry! Youth ministry, as you may have already discovered, is exciting! Seeing youth get excited about relationships, hearing about the good and bad times of their lives, "holding their hands," and helping them make life decisions are all parts of youth ministry. Helping plan programs, making mission trips, holding indepth discussions, and going on retreats are also parts of youth ministry.

One part of youth ministry that is always assumed yet often not talked about is evangelism. Somehow, congregations expect adults to teach youth all there is to know about evangelism and sharing their faith. Often the thought is, "Just teach them how to talk about Jesus Christ, and youth will automatically be able to do evangelism." Or, simply because youth attend Sunday school, church, and youth fellowship, some believe that youth are committed to Jesus Christ and are willing to talk about their faith with friends.

An underlying assumption in congregations is that evangelism is an integral and vital part of youth ministry. The problem, however, is that many adults have no clear understanding of evangelism themselves. And, while we in The United Methodist Church have been good at youth programming, adults who work with youth have not done very well in sharing their faith with youth. It is easier to talk about the faith of others than it is to talk about your own faith. We have not helped youth to understand their faith and to know how to share it.

The challenge for adults who work with youth is to achieve an understanding of what evangelism is and how to help youth develop their own understanding of evangelism. The goal of evangelism and youth ministry is to help adults claim and talk about their own faith journey as well as to help youth claim and share the faith they have found in God with their peers and family. Every church's ministry with youth must help youth find appropriate ways to share their faith. That ministry also must be undergirded and modeled by

1

adults who are supportive and who provide positive role models for the youth.

The aim of this book is to help you as an adult who works with youth to struggle with the issue of evangelism, to re-examine your own faith story, and to consider how to help youth share their faith. This is not an "instant evangelism program" or a set of ten easy steps to teach youth how to share their faith. Our intention is to take you seriously as an adult leader with youth. We hope the questions we raise and the concepts we present will cause you to rethink, reevaluate, and even redesign some of the ways you do youth ministry.

Our underlying premise about evangelism can be summed up in a simple definition. Evangelism with youth is adults relating to youth, and youth relating to youth in such a way that persons are invited into a relationship with Jesus Christ. The primary emphasis of this definition is on *relationships.* The definition includes verbal sharing of faith. We are convinced that it is important for youth and adults to be able to talk freely about their faith and relationship to God in Jesus Christ. Still, the foundation for evangelism with youth in the '90s, as we see it, is the building of relationships in which this dialogue can occur. Evangelism takes place where people are invited into relationship with Jesus Christ through relationships with others. We need to be clear: The relationship is with Jesus Christ— yet persons are most often brought into that relationship by friends. Therefore, we refer to this definition as "relational evangelism."

Larry Keefauver talks about how people become part of a Christian community. According to Keefauver, relationships are essential. He cites the following statistics to back up his claim. How do people become involved in a congregation?

- .01 percent through crusades
- 1 percent through church visitation
- 4 percent through church programs
- 4 percent through the pastor or simply by walking in
- 70 to 90 percent through the invitation of a friend[1]

Friends inviting friends. That is how many persons in the New Testament came to know Jesus Christ.

> The next day Jesus decided to go to Galilee. He found Philip and said to him, "Follow me. . . ." Philip found Nathanael and

said to him, "We have found him about whom Moses in the law and also the prophets wrote, Jesus son of Joseph from Nazareth. . . ." Nathanael replied, "Rabbi, you are the Son of God! You are the King of Israel!" (John 1:43, 45, 49).

Philip and Nathanael were friends. Philip met Jesus Christ and realized that Jesus was the Messiah. Not wanting to keep the news to himself, Philip went not to strangers, but to his friend Nathanael with the great discovery. It was after talking to Nathanael that Philip led his friend to meet Jesus. Philip led Nathanael to Jesus and introduced them. Philip did not force or coerce his friend into believing. He simply allowed Nathanael to make up his own mind.

Youth naturally want to tell their friends about significant events, people, and situations in their lives. Youth often talk for hours on the telephone about what has happened and what is happening at school, at church, and in their lives. Every parent of a teenager knows when something good (or bad) happens—the teen runs to the telephone, quickly dialing his or her best friend with the latest news. This is also how it can be when youth have a significant relationship with Jesus Christ. They tell their friends. Like Philip, many youth can and do lead their friends to know and experience the love of God and the saving grace of Jesus Christ.

Just as youth can, through their relationships, lead friends to Jesus Christ, so can you. The relationship that you and the other adults who work with youth have with the youth in your community and congregation is very important. Youth need and want relationships with adults who are loving, accepting, and caring. They respond to adults who are open and honest, who treat them with respect, and who listen carefully to what they say. Youth do not need adults who talk all the time and never give them an opportunity to express their own opinions.

Youth are searching and struggling with many questions in life— not the least of which is their relationship with God. There is nothing that turns off a young person quicker than an adult who has all the answers and is willing to tell everyone exactly what to believe and when to believe it. The last thing needed, and often the first thing rejected, is a "know-it-all" adult with all the answers.

By no means are we suggesting a style of evangelism where adults always keep silent and never share their beliefs. If adults want to be helpful and to be heard, however, they must share in a way that allows youth to question, to accept, and even to reject the beliefs offered by adults. In this sense, building the relationship is more important than saying all the right things. In an open and caring relationship, youth hear beyond the spoken words. They experience themselves as valued in this setting of hospitality.

Sometimes it is painful for caring adults to see young people struggle and reject traditional values and beliefs. This is especially true when youth are engaging in behaviors that are potentially harmful. We may not like or approve the behavior. However, if adults want to lead youth to Christ, they must be willing to accept the decisions youth make, and patiently build relationships.

Nancy is a seventeen-year-old who has been dating Bill for six months. Nancy has decided that she is in love with Bill and wants to consummate their relationship. Nancy talked with Shirley, her youth counselor, about her decision.

During the conversation, Shirley listened carefully to all of Nancy's reasons for wanting to have sexual relations with Bill. In the midst of the conversation, by asking appropriate questions, Shirley helped Nancy explore the meaning of relationships, commitment, and sexual fidelity. While they were talking, Shirley explained, in a nonjudgmental way, why she did not believe in sex before marriage. Shirley used her knowledge of scripture and what The United Methodist Church believes to support her opinion. She also shared some personal reasons and observations from her own life and work with teenagers. When the conversation was over, Shirley knew, however, that she needed to keep the open, accepting relationship she had with Nancy.

We can see the direction youth are going. We can try to help them make good decisions. Yet, they choose another path. At times, all we can do is to be there, to hold them, to dry their tears, to pick them up when they have fallen, and to assure them that they are forgiven and still loved. No matter what youth say or do, adults must be there to love them.

Picture the way God continually watches over us in love. That's a good picture of adults caring for youth. God sees the direction we are going and is often saddened with our choices. Yet, despite our choices, God continually forgives and loves us.

Inviting youth to be in relationship with Jesus Christ takes time.

Our relationship with youth, like Christ's relationship with us, is not just a Sunday event. No one is more sensitive to this than youth.
  Nothing tells youth you care about them more than being with them outside the church. If you are able, have lunch with them at school occasionally. That's right, go the extra mile, and eat the cafeteria food with them! It takes time, but if you are serious about leading youth to Jesus Christ, be with them—visit them in their homes, watch them in their sports events, support them when they are in plays, and attend their piano recitals. Be interested in their music, their movies, and their lives. What do they like or dislike? What are their hopes, their dreams, their fears, their concerns? These are all things you cannot really find out in a discussion group on Sunday. You must be with youth—one-on-one. Remember, evangelism happens in relationships.
  Touch is another dimension of youth evangelism. Almost all the miracles Jesus and his disciples did were done by touching.

> While he [Jesus] was saying these things to them, suddenly a leader of the synagogue came in and knelt before him, saying, "My daughter has just died; but come and lay your hand on her, and she will live. . . . When Jesus came to the leader's house . . . , he went in and took her by the hand, and the girl got up (Matthew 9:18, 23, 25).

> One day Peter and John were going up to the temple. . . . a man lame from birth was being carried in . . . so that he could ask for alms from those entering the temple. . . . Peter looked intently, as did John. . . . Peter said, "I have no silver or gold, but what I have I give you; in the name of Jesus Christ of Nazareth, stand up and walk." And he took him by the right hand and raised him up; and immediately his feet and ankles were made strong (Acts 3:1-7, selected verses).

As an adult who works with youth, you must be willing to touch the lives of youth. You must be willing to spend the time necessary to be with them, to know them, and to love them. You must enter into their world in order to be with them as they journey through life. Only then will you really be able to invite them into relationship with Jesus Christ.
  Take a moment now to think about your relationship with the

youth with whom you are in ministry. Do you really know "your" young people? Have you spent time with them outside of church? Are you spending time with them? List your strengths and your weaknesses in these areas.

Write down some of the changes you might need to make in order to be more open, caring, and accepting of youth.

Name some specific things you are willing to do in order to spend more quality time with your youth.

The crucial issue for adults who work with youth is to be able to show youth, *through relationships*—through words and actions— how to share the good news of Jesus Christ. Programs, pamphlets, and tracts about a loving God and saving Christ are not enough. By themselves, in fact, these can become simplistic and trite. Evangelism with youth must be done through relationships with other youth and adults who have experienced God's love and who know how to share it.

Naturally, all of this has a very *personal* side! In order to be effective models of evangelism, adults need to know God in a very personal way in their own lives. "When teachers are open to God and to other people, when they reflect a spirit of freedom and conviction, their pupils are drawn toward their teachers' faith." [2] It does no good to talk about God and the need for personal devotions and prayer in general if one does not know God and have regular devotions in one's own life. Youth are quick to spot hypocrisy in the lives of persons around them. Therefore, people who are serious about evangelism and inviting others to a relationship with Jesus Christ must experience the love of God in their own lives.

This does not mean that adults have all the answers about God. Nor does this mean that adults are always content with their relationship with God or that their faith walk is always a "mountaintop" experience. Adults need to be honest with themselves and with youth about their faith journey. It is important for adults to articulate that their relationship with God is not always the way it should be. Youth need to hear adults say that they struggle with their faith just as the youth do. An important concept to convey is that while

we all struggle, we continue to work on our relationship with God.
And, all the time, God continues to seek us!

Take a moment and think about your own relationship with God.
How is your relationship with God? In the space below list some of
the things that please you about your relationship with God.

Now, list some of the areas you feel you need to develop more fully
in order to enhance your relationship with God.

Reviewing both lists, write three things you will do to enhance or improve your relationship with God.

Think about the youth you know and with whom you are in ministry. What are some ways you can talk with them about your faith and your relationship with Jesus Christ? Write down places, situations, and ways in which you could talk with youth about your own faith. Are you willing to make a commitment to talk about your faith with one youth this week?

It is important for you as an adult to be involved in study, prayer, meditation, and worship to deepen your own faith journey. Remember, if you are going to invite youth into a relationship with Jesus Christ, you must have a relationship with Christ yourself. And, you must be ready to keep growing in your relationship with God.

In this light, the traditional means of spiritual growth and devotion have a direct relationship to your ministry with youth. Bible study, prayer, worship, and service to others are not just means for your personal growth—though they are certainly that. As an adult leader with youth, they are means to effective youth evangelism. The following are some suggestions about the means of grace that can strengthen you and sharpen your skills for relational evangelism with youth.

● *Daily Bible study that includes a specific devotional.* There are many excellent devotional guides available. Three of the most common books are: *The Upper Room Daily Devotional Guide, The Upper Room Disciplines* (both of which are daily devotional guides), and the book *A Guide to Prayer for All God's People* by Rueben Job and Norman Shawchuck. All three of these can be ordered from The Upper Room, P. O. Box 189, Nashville, Tennessee 37202 (615-340-7284). You may also want to ask your pastor, diaconal minister, or director of Christian education what he or she uses.

● *Indepth reading on spiritual formation by persons whose spiritual formation has helped others.* Great Devotional Classics (also available from The Upper Room) is a series of booklets that highlight the writings of some of the important writers on spiritual formation. Francis de Sales, Augustine, Francis Asbury, St. Francis of Assisi, and Dietrich Bonhoeffer are a few of the writers included in this series. Writings by Henri Nouwen, Mother Teresa, Howard Thurman, and Thomas Kelly also provide helpful reflection.

● *Daily prayer time.* We do not suggest that your daily prayer time be the last ten minutes of the day before you fall asleep. Rather, it is most helpful to choose any time during the day when you are able to be alone. The time you choose should also be a time when you are alert and able to concentrate on praying and on listening. You may need to find a place away from the telephone, the children, and other distractions of everyday life.

When you pray, be sure that you do not do all the talking. Prayer is not just our talking to God. It is also being quiet—listening for and to the voice of God. It is taking time to discern God's will for our life.

Many people find that their prayer life is strengthened when they join a prayer group. This group may meet early in the morning before work, sometime during the day, or even Sunday morning before Sunday school and worship. By being part of such a group, you will have an opportunity to be at one with others who share prayer concerns, who lift up the needs of others. A prayer group is a good place to lift up the names and needs of the youth with whom you work. It is also very helpful to have a prayer group undergird your whole youth ministry, including those youth who are willing to invite others into a relationship with Jesus Christ.

• *Participation in events that strengthen your spiritual life.* The United Methodist Church has several programs that are designed to aid your spiritual life. Some of these programs are: Walk to Emmaus, A Closer Walk with God: A Focus on Black Spirituality, The Academy for Spiritual Formation, and The Five-Day Academy for Spiritual Formation. These programs are open to persons of any denomination. More information can be obtained by writing to The Upper Room.

Your district and annual conference may also have specific programs to help you in your faith journey. If your annual conference has a director of spiritual formation, he or she can offer some helpful suggestions. If not, you may want to contact the annual conference board of discipleship. Ask your pastor for the name and address of the chairperson of your board.

• *Participation in weekly worship.* It is essential for every Christian to be involved regularly in worship. Worship is the place where the community of faith gathers for prayer and praise, for confession, and for hearing the Word of God read and proclaimed. It is also the place where persons are challenged to go out into the world, making the world more loving and just. If your witness to and with youth is to be heard, it is important for you to be in worship regularly. You cannot talk about how important your relationship is with God, or about the local church's youth ministry, if you are not in worship.

• *Service to others.* No book on evangelism and no discussion of growing in one's relationship with God can be complete without talking about service to our brothers and sisters. It is not enough to spend our time in prayer, in meditation, in study, and in worship if we are not involved in forms of mission outreach. Mission outreach is more than a yearly mission trip to some exotic place. Being involved in mission means that we are involved in helping those around us. Mission outreach may be serving meals at the local mission, driving cancer patients to their weekly treatments, volunteering to hold babies or children who are dying of AIDS, working with a local hospice. No matter where you live, no matter how large or how small your community is, there are always ways you can be in mission.

If we want to grow in faith, we need to hear the words of James: "Religion that is pure and undefiled before God, the Father, is this: to care for orphans and widows in their distress, and to keep oneself unstained by the world" (James 1:27). "So faith by itself, if it has no works, is dead" (James 2:17). Works of mercy and justice are part of any vital, growing faith. They are also essential to the practice of relational evangelism.

Youth ministry and evangelism is not a "one shot deal," one Sunday evening program, or a once-a-quarter event. Youth ministry and evangelism happens when adults develop relationships with youth. It grows strong as adults develop their own relationship with God. It reaches full strength as adults are willing to share their faith and lead youth to know Jesus Christ. Ministry and evangelism with youth is a relationship!

CHAPTER 2
NEW WINE FOR NEW DAYS

And no one puts new wine into old wineskins; otherwise, the wine will burst the skins, and the wine is lost, and so are the skins; but one puts new wine into fresh wineskins.
Mark 2:22

What do wine and wineskins have to do with youth, the church, and evangelism? Why use this particular set of biblical images in a book on youth and evangelism? Wine and wineskins are images that help us visualize the difficulty of finding effective ways of communicating the gospel and the love of Christ to youth in the 1990s. Adults who work with youth know that youth today do not respond to all the methods of earlier years. New days call for new ways! Jesus understood the necessity for new ways back in A.D. 30.

Picture this: You are in a small town near Lake Galilee. Jesus has been proclaiming a radical departure from the Jewish tradition and law. People are coming to question him. "Why are you eating with sinners? Why aren't you fasting like John's followers and the Pharisees? Why aren't you keeping the law of the sabbath?" The essence of Jesus' response is this: Today is a new day, and new days demand radically new ways of doing things.

To fully understand the dramatic image of Mark 2:22, in the twentieth century, we must take a journey back to a time before bottles, cans, and modern ways of fermenting wine. In the ancient process of fermenting, wine was allowed to ferment in animal skin bags. When grape juice was poured into new and flexible skins, those skins would stretch and expand with the process of fermenting. However, when the juice was poured into skins that had dried out and become inflexible, the fermenting process would tear and break the old skins. The wine would be spilled. The old, ruptured skins would be ruined. So, when the new wine, still fermenting and

expanding, was placed in the wrong containers, both the new wine
and the old wineskins were lost and ruined.

Jesus used the image of new wine in old wineskins in response to
a criticism of his teaching and example. Someone thought it was not
proper that Jesus and his disciples chose not to fast at times. Fasting
was a requirement among the sect of strict religious Jews known as
the Pharisees. They were concerned, above all else, with keeping
and observing the law—especially laws related to religious rituals.
For Jesus, however, fasting was not a requirement. He chose not to
make it a requirement for his disciples.

Jesus brought new wine and called for new wineskins. He was
not against fasting. Fasting was and is a spiritual discipline. We know
it was practiced in the early church. Jesus was, however, against the
legalisms of his day that robbed the spiritual disciplines of their
essence and power for transformation. His focus was not on the law,
but on relationships. This was a radical departure from the religious
practices at that time. But then, the gospel of Jesus is radical!

Against this historical and biblical backdrop, what can we say
about our own contemporary context? Can we use Jesus' image of
new wine in a way that is fresh and relevant for today? Is this not an
old, old story? Yes, it is. Yet, the point of the story can break in upon
each generation with newness, calling us to examine our own
religious and cultural patterns in light of the priorities of Jesus
Christ. The message of grace and the priority of relationship is the
same. But this message can and must come fresh to each of us in our
own unique setting.

There are some old wineskins—some old methods and ways
of youth ministry that were good for the new wine of relational
evangelism in their own day. But the old wineskins and methods
must not be made an end in themselves. Indeed, some of them can
only break and tear apart because they are no longer capable of
holding the new wine for a new day as it ferments, expands, and
changes. For example, there was a time when keeping youth busy
with activities was the most important part of youth ministry. Today,
however, this is not always the case. As we will see in the next
chapter, youth in the '90s long for opportunities to reflect and to
explore the meaning of life.

For you and the youth ministry of your congregation, can you think of other examples of old wineskins, old concepts that no longer relate to youth in your particular setting?

In your setting, where is the need for new wineskins—new methods, new insights, and new areas of emphasis for youth ministry?

Let's be clear. We are not talking about changing the radical nature of the gospel. The gospel has challenged individuals and world systems and brought healing, justice, and mercy to peoples across the centuries. We are, however, talking about new, fresh methods that convey the gospel to youth today—new wineskins that flex and expand in order to build relationships that invite young people into relationship with Jesus Christ.

The church has an awesome responsibility today. We must recognize changes in culture, changes in our society, and changes in youth that challenge familiar ideas. If we are to share the gospel of Jesus Christ with youth today, we must open our eyes and share in the responsibility of finding new wineskins for our day.

The Gospel of Mark was written with a sense of urgency. Mark believed that time was of the essence. Every moment was an urgent

moment in which to ask, "How are you going to respond to Jesus
Christ and the gospel?" The urgency is no less for us today. We
believe Jesus' message of hope, healing, and wholeness has rele-
vance for all persons today. This is why it is so important that we
relate to youth in ways that invite them to meet the living Christ.

Think for a moment about some typical youth of today. "William"
feels as though he has no direction in life and does not know why
he is here. He agonizes over the meaning of life for himself. "Sai" has
family in a war-torn part of the world and worries about their safety
and the world situation. "Steve," as a child, was molested by an
uncle over a period of four years. He has been deeply hurt and
needs to experience healing. "Melissa" told lies about her friend.
The stories she made up got her friend in trouble with the school
authorities. Melissa needs to experience forgiveness.

Many youth, like adults, need to know a God who loves them,
who stands with them to celebrate their joys and to cry in their
pain. There is hope. The gospel proclaims that God came into the
world in Jesus Christ. Jesus came to stand with us. He brought a
message of judgment. But this message was also a message of hope
for the future. Jesus' message of hope is that he is always with us,
and he joins us together in every age that we might be his body—
his hands and feet—to others. This is the legacy of the church in
every age.

There was a time in the history of the U.S.A. when it was the
norm for extended families to live together. Children and youth
were always around older family members. They heard stories and
learned from the faith experiences of those adults. This is no
longer true in much of our culture. More and more families are
living apart from their extended families. Children and youth are
relating to special friends of their parent or parents as substitute
uncles and aunts. In order to be the Body of Christ today, congregations are finding that they must expand their ministries to
provide adult companionship for youth. Youth ministries today
often undertake the training of large cadres of adults to become
mentors with youth, to relate to youth in honest and open ways
about the faith journey.

Likewise, there was a time when youth ministry happened almost
exclusively in the church building. Now, however, effective youth
ministry often takes place away from the church building. It may

take place in the parking lot, in the school cafeteria, in housing projects, or on the streets in the midst of drug deals and dealers.

No matter which new forms of evangelism and youth ministry you consider, there is pain in moving from the old to the new. This is so even when there is joy in the new. We remember with joy and celebration how old ways and methods touched our own lives and brought new meaning to us. We may remember the stories of our parents and other significant adults in our lives. We may want to offer those wineskins to the youth of today. We know with certainty the impact of the gospel and our relationship with God in our own lives. As a result, we are naturally prone to think that "what worked for me will work for you." This, however, is just where we need to hear Jesus' words about new wineskins.

There is a familiar story about a man who fell into a well. He called and called for help so he could get out. Finally, someone came along and threw a rope to him. He was filled to overflowing with the experience and joy of being saved and of having a second chance to live. Everyone he met, he pushed into the well so others could have the same experience he had had.

Often the assumption is that all people must have the same experience. People come to an experience with Christ in a variety of ways. This is another parable about the dangers of old "wineskins" in our ministry with youth.

Like Jesus, we need to continually be open to new ways of reaching out and forming relationships with young people today. In a subsequent chapter we shall look at some examples of contemporary youth ministries that have dared to find ways of sharing the new wine of relationship with Jesus. For now, we ask you to take some time to reflect further on where your own life and ministry are. Where are you changing and growing in order to accommodate the new wine of relational evangelism? How would you describe the presence of new wine in your life?

Where are the old wineskins in your life?

Describe some forms of religious experience or ministry that have become more form than substance for you.

Where are the new wineskins in your own spiritual journey? Describe some forms of religious experience or ministry that have recently helped you to be open to the new wine.

In what ways does the gospel make radical claims on your own life? In what ways do you see the gospel as being a radical message for our day?

How should your ministry be shaped in light of this radical gospel?

Where are the new wineskins for ministry with youth in your congregation? Name some possible ways that you might get involved in helping youth claim for themselves the radical presence of new wine.

Name some ways in which you might help youth share the new wine with each other.

CHAPTER 3
YOUTH IN THE '90S

J essica, Yvonne, Bill, Jasmine, Raul, Jorge, and Andy share a common element—they are all youth. They find living in the '90s challenging, scary, and frustrating. Youth of the '90s are surrounded by poverty, the threat of nuclear war, and the killing disease AIDS. Some of them have experimented with and are addicted to alcohol and drugs. Some are sexually active. Some of the youth have had venereal disease. Some have had abortions, or are teenage parents.

With all of these pressures and problems, however, youth still live life with an unrelenting zest. They are idealistic and strive to enjoy life. Some of today's youth are undaunted by the pressures and do not participate in at-risk behaviors. The laughter of groups of teens at the mall, the noisy halls of school, the yelling and screaming of youth as they cruise the "circuit" of their local town all give credence to the fact that many youth love life—even with its pressures, troubles, and concerns.

To be a teenager in the 1990s is to live a life that is filled with the tension of constant pressures on the one hand, and an ability to embrace life on the other.

No longer, however, do most youth live an idyllic life as depicted in the television shows of the '50s and '60s. Most teenagers do not live in the dream world of "The Donna Reed Show," "Father Knows Best," and "Leave It to Beaver."

In this chapter, we shall be talking about some of the major issues youth face today. Some readers may feel that we overstate the issues. Adults sometimes think, mistakenly, that all teenage problems are of a minor nature—Will I get a date? Will I lose weight? Should I get my hair cut? Will my voice ever change? Will my acne clear up? These are issues that affect the lives of teens. But they are not the only, or even the most prominent, issues that teens are facing today.

Search Institute, a nonprofit institute which does research to benefit children, teens and families, undertook a three-and-one-half year, indepth study of Christian education in Protestant congregations. The research included an assessment of the beliefs, behaviors, and perceptions of youth. Dr. Peter L. Benson, director of the study and president of Search Institute, developed an index to interpret the extent of "at-risk" behaviors that could block "healthy physical, psychological and spiritual development."[1] The percentages of United Methodist youth who reported one or more at-risk behaviors were:

- 7th-8th grade   64%
- 9th-10th grade   74%
- 11th-12th grade   80%

Those youth who reported three or more at-risk behaviors were:

- 7th-8th grade   9%
- 9th-10th grade   40%
- 11th-12th grade   39%[2]

As you read the following case studies and consider the statistics, you may be tempted to say, "not the youth in my church," or "not the youth in The United Methodist Church." The startling fact is, however, that these are the issues our own youth are facing. We must face them too!

Jerome is a fifteen-year-old boy who lives with his mother. Jerome sees his dad only on holidays because he lives 600 miles away. Since his parents' divorce five years ago, Jerome has come home from school to an empty house. His mother works until 6:00 in the evening. That means that Jerome must start dinner and care for his younger brother and sister until his mother comes home.

Yvonne is eighteen years old. She quit school last year so that she could work to help support her family. Her father died three years ago and left no insurance money. Her mother works as an unskilled laborer and does not make enough money to feed the family. Yvonne is not happy about the fact that she works fifty hours a week, but she must help feed and clothe her four brothers and two sisters.

Unfortunately, these stories are not uncommon. It is estimated that half of all marriages end in divorce. The number of single family households is increasing rapidly. Family stability with economic security is not the norm anymore. Families are finding that it is increasingly difficult to buy luxury items. Life's necessities—food, shelter, clothing—use up most of the families' disposable income.

Contrast this, however, with the fact that youth have more disposable income now than ever before. It is reported that teenagers earn about "$49.8 billion in disposable income each year. . . . The average annual income . . . of the 15-19 year old population is $1,893 for males and $1,796 for females."[3]

Becky is a thirteen-year-old who babysits almost every weekend. By babysitting on Friday night, sometimes Saturday afternoon or evening, and maybe a couple of times during the week, she can earn $25 to $30 per week.

Jason can earn $75 a week by working at the neighborhood fast-food restaurant. He uses the money to pay for the car he drives. While he must work about twenty-five hours a week and his grades sometimes suffer, he doesn't mind. The work is worth it when he drives around town in his "hot" car.

Bill quit school when he was fourteen. Actually he was kicked out, and he never bothered to go back. He can earn several hundred dollars a week by selling cocaine. He knows that he may eventually be caught and sent to jail, but he is addicted to his habit. Besides, what other job will pay a sixteen-year-old $400 a week?

Disposable income among teenagers and the need to help support their families are critical issues for youth. People in advertising are keenly aware of the amount of disposable income youth have. The media have become quite adept at tempting youth with various products.

Jessica and Andy have been dating for two years. They love each other and plan to marry when they both graduate from high school in two years. They have been sexually active for six months and practice birth control.

Jerry is a senior in high school. He is active in sports and plays first base on the baseball team. For the past year and a half, Jerry has struggled with the fact that he thinks he is gay. His life is made more difficult because he feels that he has no one to talk to about his feelings.

Elizabeth is getting ready to graduate from high school. She has made a decision that she will not be sexually active until she gets married. While she is satisfied with that decision, it is not always easy to stick to her commitment.

The '90s find youth struggling with the issue of sexuality more than ever. While the data vary, all statistics point to the fact that more teenagers are sexually active than ever before. Not only are they sexually active, many are not practicing reliable means of birth control. In fact, one study suggests that "approximately 50% do not use contraceptives at first intercourse, and half of premarital pregnancies occur within the first 6 months after sexual initiation. Eleven percent of adolescent girls become pregnant each year, and 4% have an abortion."[4]

While teenage pregnancy is on the rise, so are the reported cases of AIDS among older teens and young adults. Many studies now suggest that more teens than first thought are infected with the HIV virus. *Youthworker Update* reports:

> There is a growing evidence that teenagers are among the high-risk groups that are in danger of contracting the AIDS virus. A study of over a million teenagers who applied to enlist in the U.S. Army during the past four years revealed that one in 3000 were infected with AIDS, and a recent *Seventeen* article reported that about a quarter of the ten thousand women who have been diagnosed with AIDS are in their 20s, as are about 20% of the one-hundred thousand men. Which means that many if not most of men and women became infected while they were still in their teens.[5]

Jerry's concern about the possibility of being gay raises a difficult issue for the church. Homosexuality often raises heated debate whenever it is discussed. Regardless of the debate, adults who work with youth need to understand the pain of youth who are struggling with sexual identity issues.

> The report of the Health and Human Services' Task Force on Youth Suicide indicated that "gay and lesbian youth face extreme physical and verbal abuse, rejection, and isolation from families and peers. They often feel totally alone and socially withdrawn out of fear of adverse conditions."[6]

Bart is a junior in high school who enjoys a good time. Part of his definition of a good time is to be able to gather with his friends and drink beer. Bart often drinks eight to ten beers an evening.

Julie also enjoys a good time and being able to party with her friends. She chooses not to drink. Because of the choice she has made, Julie is the designated driver for her friends.

Raul is good in sports and excels at weightlifting. His goal is to be able to be on the United States Olympic weightlifting team. To help increase his strength, Raul has been taking steroids. They have really helped, and he hopes that he can stop taking them soon.

Jasmine uses cocaine occasionally. She enjoys the feeling it gives her—and it helps to dull the hassles she gets from her parents. Jasmine is not concerned about using cocaine because she believes she can stop any time she wants.

Alcohol and substance use and abuse by teenagers is not uncommon. Statistics suggest that substance abuse may be slightly declining. However, alcohol use among teenagers is not. The Gallup Study of America's Youth suggests that 16 percent of teenagers ages thirteen to fifteen use alcohol, while 37 percent of youth ages sixteen to seventeen report using alcohol.[7]

Another study, reported in the *Youth Ministry Resource Book*, says:

> Alcohol is widely available to high schoolers. Seventy-seven percent of high-achieving juniors and seniors say using alcohol is part of students' regular weekend activity. Seventy-one percent report alcohol is common at student-hosted parties, while 38 percent say it's available at school-sponsored activities. And 19 percent report that some students use alcohol in the morning before school.[8]

When Billy gets home from school, he never knows what kind of mood his dad will be in. Sometimes he finds him in a good mood, and life is pretty good. However, when his dad is in a bad mood, watch out. Billy often gets called all kinds of names and his dad hits him a lot.

Susan is thirteen and scared to be alone with her Uncle Bob. He often makes subtle remarks about her developing body and touches her inappropriately. Several times he has forced her to do things she didn't want to do. She can't fight him, and she feels no one would believe her if she tried to tell others what has happened.

Child and youth abuse, whether physical, sexual, or emotional, is on the rise in the United States. According to the American Humane Association, 2.1 million children and youth up to eighteen years of age were *reported* abused in 1986. Of the actual substantiated abuse cases, 24 percent were between the ages of twelve and seventeen. They further reported that from 1976 to 1987, the total number of abused or neglected children (up to eighteen years of age) increased 225 percent.[9]

For the past two years, Jimmy had been unhappy. Even though he was a track star, honor roll student, and president of his youth group, he felt that he wasn't good enough. One day, he couldn't stand the pressure any more. He ended his life.

Jennifer's boyfriend, Jorge, broke up with her. He was everything to her—her whole life. She could not understand, accept, or cope with the idea that he no longer loved her. One evening, Jennifer surrounded herself with all the pictures and presents Jorge had given her, and she swallowed several pills. Fortunately, her father found her and she received medical help in time. Because her father was one of the prominent clergy in town, the near suicide was never reported.

According to statistics, teen suicide has tripled in the last thirty years.[10] "Suicide is now the second leading cause of death among adolescents aged 15 to 19. . . . As many as 4% of high school students have made a suicide attempt within the previous 12 months, and 8% have made a suicide attempt sometime in their life."[11] These statistics do not take into account the thousands of attempted teen suicides that are never reported.

Pam has a problem seeing herself as a person of worth. She believes that there is nothing attractive or good about herself. Pam is not unlike thousands of teens who suffer from low self-esteem and/or deep feelings of loneliness. In his latest studies Merton Strommen found that "approximately one in five church youth are troubled by low self-regard and feelings of loneliness."[12]

Youth within the church are not immune to the pressures of the 1990s. For a variety of reasons, many of our youth are searching for meaning in life through drugs and alcohol, sexual release, and suicide. Many of our youth are plagued by feelings of self-doubt, unworthiness, and even self-hatred.

Recognizing and coming to grips with the kinds of problems youth today are facing is not an easy task. In fact, it is all too easy to feel overwhelmed, and to want to withdraw and hide from the problems. Still, if the church is to create new wineskins, new forms of ministry that truly connect with the needs of youth today, then we as adults who work with youth must face squarely the problems youth face. While it is uncomfortable and painful, and sometimes fills us with fear, this is the arena in which God has called us to work. In the last five years violence among the teen population has increased dramatically. Youth carrying weapons to school, settling arguments by violence and force, are no longer primarily associated with the inner city. The issue of violence and teens is an increasing concern for the church and for adults who work with youth.

Think about the youth with whom you minister. Visualize each one. What are the pressures each is facing? What things concern, scare, and frustrate them? List some of those things in the space below.

Now think about your own life—your pressures, fears, and frustrations. List some of these.

In Chapter 2 we talked about the importance of a relationship with God. How has your relationship with God helped you cope with the pressures, fears, and frustrations of your life? Write some notes about this here.

Evangelism with youth means establishing relationships with them so that you can honestly and openly share your faith journey. It means helping youth see who God is, and how God supports us every day. Youth ministry and evangelism means helping youth see God through Christ in you and in your daily life. One of the best ways you have to invite youth into relationship with Jesus Christ is to share your own story.

In closing this chapter, we as authors want to share some of the basic biblical principles that have sustained us—both in our own lives and in our ministries with youth. We believe that scripture and experience have important, life-changing things to say to the youth with whom we work. In the words of the old hymn, "We've a story to tell." This story can stand against the pressures and pitfalls of life in the '90s. Yet, the story must also be told with freshness, newness, and authenticity. And it must be proclaimed loudly and boldly. You must find the ways to share it with your youth.

God is active! The God of the Old and New Testaments is a God who was active in the lives of the people. The scriptures tell over and over of God's active involvement with the people God created. This God of history is also the God of today. God is active today in the world and in people's lives. Our faith bears witness to a God who is intervening in the world. God is not some far-off being who has nothing to do with us. Rather, the God of Abraham and Sarah and of Jacob and Rebekah is also the God of Pam, Jasmine, Jerry, and Yvonne.

Youth need to know and to understand that God is an active God who is interested and involved in their lives. Adults can model and guide youth as the adults give verbal witness to what God has done and continues to do in their own lives.

God can make a difference in lives! There is a yearning, a searching in all of us for meaning in life, for a sense of purpose. This is especially true for teens as they develop, grow, and mature. In the '90s persons are searching in a variety of places and in a variety of ways to find meaning.

We in the church believe that God through Christ can give meaning and purpose to life. It is through understanding God's love and purpose for our lives and through living in joyful obedience to God's will that we find meaning. Teens need to discover that obedience to God is not really a limiting of one's freedom, but a way into true meaning and happiness. They need to see this in the lives of adults.

God expects commitment! The scriptures are clear: Jesus continually called people to commitment. Sometimes they responded; sometimes they did not. Nonetheless, Jesus continued to call for commitment.

Adults who work with youth must understand that God expects a commitment from us. The commitment begins with accepting Jesus Christ. It continues with decisions about how we live our life and how we respond to the needs of those around us.

Adult leaders with youth must teach, through word and example, that God expects total commitment. It is not easy, nor is it always safe when we commit ourselves to God. But God expects commitment. And young people have an inherent respect for adults who are truly committed.

When students join the band or a sports team, commitment is

essential. Coaches and directors are quick to point out the sacrifices that will need to be made. They are not ashamed to insist on the sacrifices—hours of practice, long drills in the hot sun, lost sleep, and sore muscles. Yet, students commit themselves mind, body, and spirit to it. Young people are searching for something worthy of their faithfulness.

As churches work with youth and evangelism, we must hold before youth the understanding that God expects commitment. The commitment that God expects is total, and there are expectations that come with it. No longer can we offer youth an easy, lukewarm, mild-mannered possibility of commitment to God in Christ. "As long as the churches continue to present the issues of discipleship in a context they [youth] find relatively manageable and unthreatening, youth will fail to find sufficient scope there for their very considerable zeal. We should not be surprised, then, if they look elsewhere."[13]

Youth in the '90s face a great deal of stress as they live life. If the church is to be a relevant force in their lives, it is imperative that we understand their pressures and their life. We need to be willing to be with youth — supporting them, nurturing them, and offering them the love of God. We also must be willing to give witness to our faith. Our life needs to be a life that is lived with commitment to God.

For youth to be led to Christ and to live a life in the awareness of God's love, they must see, hear, and know the God of covenant and commitment. This awareness of God transcends programs, workshops, and movies on evangelism. The meaning of commitment is caught—not taught. It must be lived by word and deed.

> Ultimately, the spiritual needs of youth transcend the legitimate requirements of wholesome companionship, entertaining events, and even worthwhile service projects. What they ask from the church is not so much something to do as something to be. . . . The fundamental need they have to commit themselves body and soul to some One who will ask everything in return goes unrecognized by adults who themselves have been asked to give "much" but not all.[14]

CHAPTER 4
OLD WINESKINS: Myth-Conceptions
about Adults and Youth

Myth-Conceptions about Adults

> *Myth-Conception:* Adults have all the answers.
> Faith comes tied up in a neat box with a pretty
> bow.

Sometimes adults feel that, in order to work with youth, they must project an image of having everything perfectly together. This is a misconception for several reasons.

First, Christianity is not simply a particular set of beliefs or doctrines. At the deepest level, Christianity is about relationships. It is about growing in the likeness of Christ. When we have stopped growing, we have died. If we are to model this process of growth to youth, then it is not necessary for adults to have all the answers. It is imperative that adults be vulnerable. Workers with youth don't need all the answers, but they need to be honest and open. For adults to model their own questioning, their own process of growth and change in the Christian faith is one of the most effective ways to assure youth that it is okay for them to raise questions. This process will help teens see Christianity as growth in relationship to God and in likeness to Christ.

To be vulnerable to one another is also to model the biblical virtue of hospitality which values all persons. Abraham and Sarah were open to hearing a message from strangers. In doing so they received a gift from God (news of the coming birth of a child). To practice hospitality is to relax in the presence of another person so that we can receive a message or a gift from God through that person. The virtue of hospitality teaches us to value teens as persons and to expect to learn from them. There is mutuality in our relationship with teenagers. Such a posture of vulnerability and receptivity is quite the opposite of an attitude in which one has all the answers.

Another side of Christian hospitality is sharing. As Christians we are called to share with each other as though we are sharing with the living Christ. Therefore, we relate to teens as though we are relating to the living Christ. What a difference this makes.

> *Myth-Conception:* I don't have a dynamic story. Therefore, it is not essential to share my faith story.

One of the most harmful things we can do in the Christian church is to imply that every Christian must have a story like that of Saul on the Road to Damascus (Acts 9:1-19; 22:6-16; 26:12-18). When we do this, we leave the impression that one may not be Christian at all unless one has this kind of dynamic and dramatic conversion experience. As a result, when we finally do invite persons to tell their stories in the church, they are often afraid to share unless their stories are highly dramatic: the young person who was on drugs and had to steal to keep his habit going; the young woman who was critically injured in an accident but who was miraculously healed, etc. Our attitude to such stories can continue to foster the myth-conception, for adults as well as for teens, that "your story must be dramatic for it to be worth hearing."

In reality, the essence of Christian faith stories is simple: Christ in our lives. Such stories tell of a journey with the living Christ, and of growing into the likeness of Christ. These kinds of stories are essential in the lives of all Christians. But they are not necessarily dramatic, nor do they have to be.

Search Institute found that only 6 percent of the adults surveyed in The United Methodist Church report a specific moment of conversion. Other adults report gradual experiences of coming to faith in Christ.[1] Witnessing to a faith journey that does not have "dramatic" content models the validity of such a witness for those with similar experiences in life. All of us need to know that our own stories can and do intersect with God's story.

Myth-Conception: I don't know scripture well enough to share faith. I should be a biblical scholar in order to be in ministry with youth.

The good news is: God accepts you where you are in your Christian journey. There is no "critical mass" of knowledge that qualifies one to be in ministry with youth or anyone else. It is not what you don't, but what you *do* know that God can use. What are the biblical stories you know? How can you explore the meaning of the Bible more fully? Trust your own experience. What are the biblical stories you have heard that have captured your attention? List three or four that come to mind immediately.

Have there been times in your life when the Bible had special meaning for you? Have there been times when the Bible, or some-

thing in the Bible, became a real problem for you? Describe some of
your experiences.

The place to begin with the Bible is always right where you are.
(This is true for preachers too.) Then, if you want to improve your
understanding in some ways, there are some things you can do. Do
you have a daily time of personal devotion and Bible reading? There
is no better way to become acquainted with the Bible than to read
it. Are there study groups in your congregation or community that
you could join? Discussing the Bible with others is always a great
way to learn. In addition, you might want to ask your pastor or
other staff person for suggestions about a study plan. It is often
helpful to have a plan for studying the scripture.

Whatever you do, don't fall prey to the myth-conception of
academic qualification. God has spoken in the past through the
scriptures. God continues to speak to people through the Bible.
Our lives are drawn closer to the living God as we "hear" the
biblical accounts for ourselves.

In ministry, you have to share from the point where you are now.
When we learn to swim, we don't stay on land studying the books
until we think we're ready to compete in the Olympics. We practice
swimming! Practice sharing your faith at the point where you are in
your faith journey. As you allow yourself to be formed spiritually
through worship, spiritual disciplines, and service, you will become
a different person. The change may occur in the next several years, or
maybe in the next few days and weeks. Others will also learn from
you as you are honest about your own struggles. If you have not been
studying scripture regularly, it is important to begin. If you have been
studying the scripture, keep growing and going forward in your
study.

Myth-Conception: Adults can teach spirituality
and faith. I can read a book or go to a workshop
on evangelism and then teach it.

As we said earlier, Christianity is not simply doctrine or information. It is a matter of relationships and a way of life. We can teach
about the faith. We can teach about spirituality. Studies have shown,
however, that most people will not embrace faith simply as a
transfer of information from one person to another. As an adult
leader with youth, be careful not to spend all of your devotional and
meditation time in reading *about* God or in reading *about* spirituality. There is a saying in *Desert Wisdom:* "Abba Sisoes said: Seek
God, and not where God lives."[2]

One of the best ways to grow as a Christian is through a mentoring
relationship with another person. Spirituality takes hold of us like a
story that awakens our imagination and vision. We see afresh who we
are and who God is. By offering, inviting, and telling faith stories, you
can help youth come to the place of claiming faith for themselves.
Adult leaders with youth are called to walk arm in arm with youth as
all of us continue our faith journeys, each at different stages.

We do not learn faith simply from a book. Faith development is a
process. At times, like people in the biblical stories, we are sure of
our convictions. We confidently proclaim that we will never deny
Christ. We will never make a decision that is not faithful to the
Christ. Then, in a moment of human weakness, we fail. We agonize
over our unfaithfulness. We remember Peter who boldly proclaimed he would never deny Christ. We remember the disciples
who ran when they thought their lives were in danger. We remember the two "beloved" disciples who could not even stay
awake while Jesus prayed that last evening. We remember our
humanness, and we remember also the hope that we see in the
biblical account as the disciples continued to grow—continued to
share the good news even after those moments of weakness. So,
sometimes we are marching forward. And sometimes, it seems, we
are going backward. But together we can encourage and pray for
one another in our faith journeys that we might continue to grow in
our relationship to the living Christ.

> *Myth-Conception:* My major concern is not my
> own spirituality, because I am saved. My major
> concern is the youth and their faith journey.

As Christians, all of us are concerned about opening our lives to
the wholeness of the gospel. We know that our response to the
grace of God influences everything about us—how we live, how we
make decisions, how we relate to others, and how we invite others
into the faith journey. To grow in Christian faith is to become more
and more clear that faith itself is a constant intertwining of our
openness to God and our openness to the world—to people and all
of creation.

As a consequence, we never reach a point in the Christian life
where we have "arrived." Though we long deeply for teens to have
a relationship with the living Christ, our own journey never ends. In
fact, as we have been saying in many different ways, sharing our
own journey is one of the best ways to have a truly positive
influence in the lives of young people.

> *Myth-Conception:* My *primary* responsibility is
> to help young people be "moral."

In *Resident Aliens,* Stanley Hauerwas and Will Willimon address
this myth directly: " . . . ethics is first a way of *seeing* before it is a
matter of *doing.* The ethical task is not to tell you what is right or
wrong, but rather to train you to see."[3] We are called to invite youth
to be a part of a people who see with different eyes—who see the
world in ways that may be very different than that of culture or
society. Harold Kushner, in *Who Needs God?*, writes, "Religion has to
mean more to us than a commitment to ethical behavior, to loving
our neighbors. It has to teach our eyes how to see the world."[4]

If we could see with the eyes of Christ, how would we see
people? How would we see homeless youth, youth who are gay or
lesbian, youth who are poor, youth who are pregnant? How would
we see the issues of the world? How would we see relationships? As
we grow in discipleship and in our relationship to God, perhaps we

too will receive new sight and new ways of seeing all of God's world. "Youth whose lives are rooted in faith, who live in awareness of God's promises, show an inner power that becomes evident in their behavior,"[5]

Myth-Conceptions about Youth

> *Myth-Conception:* Youth are not concerned about spiritual growth.

This myth is a good example of an "old wineskin," an outdated idea about youth and evangelism. Often adults are heard to say, "Youth don't really care about growing in Christ." Or, "The youth I work with couldn't care less about a relationship with Jesus Christ." This may have been true at some time in history, but it is not true today.

It is true that *some* youth are not concerned about spiritual growth. Part of the reason for this is that adults often present issues of spiritual growth, Bible study, and prayer in very boring, "ho-hum" ways. Some adults themselves think these issues are boring because they are not of primary importance in the lives of some adults.

The new wine of youth ministry is that significant numbers of youth are taking spiritual growth and evangelism very seriously. Search Institute discovered in their *Effective Christian Education* study that youth "give high rank to . . . learning about the spiritual life."[6] Small groups of youth are meeting regularly around the country for Bible study, prayer, and times of study around spiritual growth issues. Youth meet during school (when permissible), after school, and in the evening.

The new wine of Jesus Christ and the Word of God is relevant for the youth of today. Many of the youth of today want to find ways to study, to meditate, and to learn. Adult leaders of youth must find the new wineskins—new ways of helping youth grow in faith.

> *Myth-Conception:* All youth want is to have fun, food, and fellowship.

This myth is the flipside of the preceding one. Youth do enjoy fun and games. Times of recreation and unstructured activity are important. They are important especially in our fast-paced, frenzied world. Many youth are overcommitted overachievers who try too hard to grow up too quickly. Youth need times that allow them to be youth. They need opportunity for playing, for running, and for just having fun.

Becky, Allison, and Keith are members of a medium-sized church. There are about forty-five youth on the rolls of the church. The UMYF, which meets regularly, has about twenty-three youth who attend. Most of the programs consist of water-balloon volleyball, scavenger hunts, and watching the television in the youth room.

These three youth wanted more than games on Sunday evening. When they began to talk to other youth, they discovered that they were not the only ones who felt this way. Their comment was "we can play those games in other groups we are in. We assumed that UMYF would be different from just a social club."

Youth need and want to belong to a group that is more than a social and recreational club.

> Youth ministry should provide opportunities for youth that they would not or probably could not have with the other groups they belong to. . . . Many youth are getting their recreational needs met elsewhere and will probably not attend or be especially excited about another group that features [only] recreation.[7]

The new wineskins of youth ministry are those activities and programs that provide significant, meaningful opportunities for spiritual life and growth. For youth ministry to be of value, it must provide ways for youth to relate to God, to be nurtured in the faith, and to be involved in service to their community and world.

> *Myth-Conception:* Youth only need one invitation to make a commitment to Jesus Christ. If the gospel is represented correctly, every youth will immediately respond.

Beth is a frustrated adult leader with youth. She works hard at helping youth develop exciting, relevant programs for Sunday evening youth fellowship. They recently had an excellent program on making a commitment to Jesus Christ. Many of the youth commented how good the program was. Beth's concern was that no one came forward to make an actual commitment to Jesus Christ.

Beth responded like many of us would have. She wanted results instantly! The gospel of Jesus Christ is good news. We expect all who hear it to understand that the news is good for them. They should receive it immediately.

Beth is also a product of the '90s. People in the '90s often feel that things can be solved, resolved, and accomplished in a short period of time. Television plots are finished in half an hour. People's lives are changed, relationships healed, and success gained in a two-hour movie.

Helping youth make commitments to Jesus Christ is not a one-shot deal. As we have stated earlier, commitment requires more than one program, one revival, or one late-night talk. Commitment is, or should be, the foundation of every youth program.

In looking at this myth, we want to suggest a particular new wineskin that is worthy of your consideration. Find ways with your youth to emphasize the importance of commitment to Jesus Christ. Persons who work with youth must present the idea of commitment over and over in many different ways. Youth are used to hearing things in a variety of ways, and commitment to Jesus Christ is no different.

Adult leaders with youth should not get discouraged if youth do not respond as the adults feel they should. Adults must take responsibility for inviting, but not for the results. It is essential that adults be willing to leave the results in God's hands. God calls persons to faithfulness, not to results. The role for adult leaders with youth is to be faithful to the task of inviting youth to a deeper relationship with Jesus Christ.

Another feature to bear in mind about this new wineskin is that youth, like adults, respond to commitment in a variety of ways. All youth do not respond immediately. Response to the gospel invitation for some may be an immediate yes. Other youth may need some time to think about the invitation, to weigh the options, and to consider everything before they respond. In any case, some youth will hear the invitation and say, "No way!"

It is difficult in youth ministry to allow youth the space to say, "No way." Hearing that response can be discouraging. Yet, we must realize how often we say no to God. God does not, however, give up on us. Adults who work with youth can do no less!

> *Myth-Conception:* Once youth have accepted Jesus Christ, they will automatically go out and tell others about him.

This myth is great in theory but terrible in practice. Part of being a youth is wanting to fit in with a peer group. The need to be different (from adults), yet like friends, is part of peer group acceptance. Youth, like adults, need and want to be accepted.

Many youth (and adults) have a significant relationship with God through Christ, yet they do not always share their faith with others. There are several reasons why youth do not always tell their friends about Jesus Christ. Some of these reasons are:

- They are afraid their friends will reject them, laugh at them, or make fun of them.
- They do not know how to talk about their faith.
- They have not had good role models of faith sharing.
- They feel other youth may not want to hear about God.

The first step in helping youth share their faith is to understand the reasons why youth find it difficult to talk about God. Maybe you can think of some additional reasons why youth find it hard to share their faith.

A new wineskin in this regard would be to help youth develop strategies and programs for genuine faith sharing. As we have pointed out, youth need good, consistent role models to show them how to share their faith. Adults who work with youth must show by example that it is possible to share faith with friends and to talk about spiritual things in a natural way.

Youth need to understand that sharing faith is not easy. For many persons, it is one of the most difficult things to do. Sharing faith is sharing a very personal part of ourselves. Sharing faith also leaves us open and vulnerable to ridicule and rejection. Ongoing programs and conversations about how to respond to ridicule and rejection have proved very helpful to many young people.

Adult leaders must also help youth *practice* sharing their faith. Programs that give examples of sharing faith are helpful. Practice sessions of sharing faith through role plays and short dramas are also helpful. Such programs can help youth become more comfortable in sharing their faith journey.

Youth also need time to talk about their experiences of trying to share their faith. Provide opportunities for youth to talk about their experiences—both positive and not so positive. Allow times for youth to voice their frustrations, fears, and concerns. The skilled adult leader who listens can help youth find renewed strength to continue sharing their story with others.

> *Myth-Conception:* Once a youth receives Jesus Christ, we no longer have to worry about that individual. We can move on to other youth.

One day a youth pastor was at an amusement park with a youth group. Several youth and the pastor went on a particularly scary ride. One of the youth exclaimed, "We're glad you're along. We're safe since you're a minister."

The youth gave expression to the basic assumption of this myth: Once someone accepts Jesus Christ, life is perfect and safe. Many adults who work with youth feel that once Johnny, Jane, or Maria has a significant relationship with Jesus Christ, then all is well. No longer does the leader need to be concerned with that youth's self-esteem, moral decisions, or faith journey. Simply because the youth has made a commitment, life will fall into place and there will be no more troubles, worries, or anxieties.

Having a relationship with Jesus Christ does not automatically make life fall into place. Recognizing the need for God in one's life is not some magical prescription for a carefree life.

Youth who accept Jesus Christ still have questions about self-esteem. Youth who have an ongoing relationship with God still have questions about whether to have sex or not. Youth who are working on their faith journey are still subject to large amounts of peer pressure.

It is important to remember the words of the Apostle Paul when he said, "I do not understand my own actions. For I do not do what I want, but I do the very thing I hate" (Romans 7:15). Youth of today are no different from the Apostle Paul.

> *Myth-Conception:* Once young people accept Jesus Christ, they will automatically be open to other youth. A youth group that strives for an ongoing relationship with God will not have cliques.

In his book, *Friends & Faith,* Larry Keefauver tells about a youth group he worked with. He knew the members of the group really loved Christ and one another. Everyone fit in and accepted everyone else. One evening, Larry invited Debra to the group. That evening, one person teased her about her weight and none of the girls talked with her. Debra never came back. Larry says, "I had assumed that because they had accepted Christ, evangelism would be automatic. . . . I had to take some important steps to help us grow from a selfish youth group to a caring one."[8]

Like adults, youth do not always reach out to others. Youth groups have cliques. They have small groups that often exclude others. Helping youth reach beyond the cliques is not easy.

Just because the youth with whom you work have a relationship with God, don't assume that they will automatically be open to others. An open, caring youth group, Sunday school class, and/or Bible study group does not just happen. It takes lots of work and constant nurturing.

Making a new wineskin for the openness and hospitality of the Spirit means finding ways to move beyond the cliques in openness and vulnerability to others. Jesus was constantly reminding his disciples that they must accept others. Even when his disciples tried to keep persons away, Jesus' response was, "Let them come to me." As adults who work with youth, we can help our youth groups learn what it means to say, "Let them come to us!"

CHAPTER 5
OLD WINESKINS: MYTH-CONCEPTIONS
ABOUT EVANGELISM

Just as there are "myth-conceptions" about youth and adults, there are also myths about evangelism. Making room for the new wine of the Spirit requires new forms of evangelism.

> *Myth-Conception:* Evangelism has to do with only a part of life—the "spiritual" or the "religious" part. But evangelism doesn't really affect all of life. Faith belongs in its own compartment. You can be a "Sunday Christian."

The new wine has broken in upon us. Actually, the new wine broke in upon the world in the time of the early church. The early Christians knew there was a cost in being part of the people of the Way. In some cases, they lost relationships with family and friends as they identified with Jesus the Messiah. For some, allegiance to Christ meant persecution by the authorities. Christian faith was a way of life. Faith affected everything—the way one lived and the way one related to family, friends, neighbors, strangers, and the environment.

The new wine of Jesus' Spirit needs to break in upon us today and capture our total being! We must help youth catch the vision of new wine—affecting their whole life, every decision, every action they make in daily living. The decisions are not always easy. Some decisions may mean going against the cultural norms of the day. But the new wine, the living Christ, invites us to live in terms of the kingdom in all of life. The center of our faith is Christ. As workers with youth, our own lifestyle needs to model wholeness. Our own faith journey cannot be compartmentalized.

> *Myth-Conception:* The best form of evangelism
> for youth is to have them make posters for
> events, serve meals, and do the babysitting for
> all church functions. When youth get involved
> in supporting the adult ministries of the con-
> gregation, they are fully involved in evangelism.

The new wine of Jesus' Spirit moves us to carefully examine the
way we treat all persons. We are called to examine our motivation for
asking persons to serve in specific ways. To be sure, we need posters
for publicity. No doubt we need persons to serve meals for functions.
Congregations with young families are always in need of child care
so everyone can participate in the activities and ministries.

The question that must be raised is, "What is our motivation for
asking youth to share in these particular responsibilities?" Are we
sometimes "dumping on youth" those things which we, as adults,
do not want to do? Are we really being honest that our motivation is
to involve them? Have we taken the time to talk with them, to
discern the best ways to fully involve them in the programming of
the church?

We need to break open the old wineskin of expectations about
youth involvement in the congregation. We need to see the full
flourishing of what youth ministry and evangelism can actually become. Ministries of serving and helping need to be shared across
generational lines—both to allow *all* ages to participate in programs and also to place more adults in contact with more youth in
all kinds of settings. Youth need to see adults who model the ministry of serving. And youth also need to know that their presence
matters in other forms of ministry, such as teaching and worship.

The new wineskin of intergenerational forms of involvement in
every area of ministry speaks loudly and clearly to youth. They are
full participants in the ministry of God. As these forms of ministry
take shape, moreover, other youth will recognize that something
new and different is taking place. That's the way of new wine.

As for the importance of ministries of service, we recall the story
of the gathering of the disciples with Jesus in the upper room
(John 13). They gathered for what would be their last Passover meal

together. As they gathered, their feet were dirty from walking the dusty roads in their sandals. The custom of the day was for the host to wash the feet of the guests as they arrived from their journey. The disciples gathered, but no one showed the common courtesy to the others. Then, in the midst of eating, at the wrong time, Jesus poured water in a basin. He put a towel around his waist and knelt in front of the disciples to wash their feet. The teacher, the leader, the savior knelt to wash the feet of his disciples.

Then, do you remember what happened? Peter refused to let Jesus wash his feet. He probably thought he was doing the right thing. Jesus should not share in a servant's role. "Not my feet. You're not going to wash my feet." But Jesus responded, "Unless I wash your feet, you have no part of me." At the close of that time Jesus reminded the disciples that no one is greater than another. He had set an example for them that they should also wash one another's feet.

Allow the new wine to pour into the new wineskins. What are the ways in which youth and adults can wash one another's feet and receive the gift of the footwashing from one another?

> *Myth-Conception:* A good way to build the youth group is to increase the numbers. Focus on numbers and do anything we can to get more people into the group. Evangelism means growing in numbers.

This myth can quickly give way to the assumption that any gimmick is acceptable as long as we grow in numbers. The youth minister becomes the pied piper or the entertainer. At the same time, the focus on real ministry and significant spiritual growth can become blurred.

The new wine of Jesus' Spirit leads us to a different focus. The focus is not on numbers per se but upon how to reach out to youth, to receive them, to help them discover their relationship with the living Christ, and then to help them find their place of service and discipleship in the world.

Look around. Where are the youth in your area hurting? What are the issues that confront them? What are the places of tension for them? How can the church offer new wine in new wineskins, so

that the hurts may be healed, the tough decisions faced, the issues
of life vested with new meaning and hope?

Evangelism means sharing the good news of Jesus Christ by
inviting others into relationship with him. As youth and their leaders concern themselves with the real needs of other youth—both
inside and outside the congregation—the numbers will take care of
themselves. In this sense, numbers are more a result than a cause of
ministry. Be assured: Where new wineskins of genuine ministry are
provided, the new wine will expand to fill them.

> *Myth-Conception:* Evangelism is an optional
> topic for youth meetings. The topic can be sched-
> uled into the program from time to time. One
> Sunday evening program or one six-week session
> on evangelism and faith sharing is enough.

Evangelism is not optional! Evangelism, sharing the good news of
Jesus Christ, is not a "program" we can decide to have this year and
not next. Evangelism is what the church is all about.

The Christian faith is relational. Faith is a relationship to God and
to the living Christ. It is a way of relating to one another and to the
world so that God's dream of shalom, peace, and wholeness can be
seen in all persons and in all creation. This is not an option in the
Christian faith. It is not an option in any of our ministries. Helping
persons relate to the living God and grow in this faith is a part of all
we do. In reality, evangelism must undergird all we do. Certainly,
there are times when we are more intentional about helping persons
share their faith and when we help youth understand evangelism. But
the modeling and encouraging and inviting are a part of all we do.

> *Myth-Conception:* It is not important to connect
> my personal story with the biblical story when
> sharing my faith. This myth takes two forms: "It is
> not necessary to share my faith journey; it is only
> important to tell the truths and stories of the
> Bible." "It is not necessarily important to tell
> Bible stories; it is most important to tell my faith
> story as I witness to others about Christ."

Stories are an important part of our lives. Stories are a vital part of the Christian faith. According to Jim Fleming, a New Testament scholar, storytelling was an integral part of faith and tradition in the ancient Mediterranean world where the Bible was written. In both the Old and the New Testaments, stories are one of the main ways of sharing faith. In this biblical tradition, the chief concern is not to remember all the details of the story. What is important is to remember who God is and what God has done, so that the truth of the story, its very essence, can be passed along.

Stories of personal faith, along with stories from the scripture, have power to transform lives. Peter Morgan in *Story Weaving* says:

> We can understand evangelism as helping persons outside the faith weave their stories into God's story in such a way that they freely respond in faith and participation in the church. Outreach is important. We can understand vital participation in the church as weaving our stories and the stories of people of faith with the biblical stories in such a way as to empower God's mission for the church. Christian community is important. The biblical story is basic.[1]

We need to be able to tell the stories of the Bible. Yet we also need to be able to tell these stories in such a way that youth can identify with the essentials. Remember the story of Moses and the people wandering in the wilderness? When in your life have you wandered in the wilderness, wondering where the end was, uncertain if you had been forsaken by God, questioning if it was necessary to remain faithful to your God in light of all that was happening around you?

Jacob was on his way from Beersheba to Haran. It was night, so he found a stone to use for a pillow under his head. In the night he had a dream. God spoke to him and blessed him. Jacob awoke, very certain of the presence of God in that place and assured of God's presence on his journey (Genesis 28:10-22). Have you ever experienced the presence of God in a dream in such a vital way that you awoke, transformed by God's presence with you?

How can you learn to connect the biblical story with your personal story? At its best, this is what scripture reading and meditation are all about. As we are able to see how our own faith journeys intersect with God's story and the stories of faith, we will be better able to share faith with youth. Youth leaders can model for young people what it means to identify with the characters and the situations of the biblical stories.

In the Gospel of John we read the story of the woman at the well. Jesus stopped at a well and asked for a drink. After he and the woman had a conversation, she went back to the people. She told them to come and see the one who had told her everything about her life. She had met Jesus and she invited others to meet him as well. At the end of this story, the people no longer believed because of what she had said, but they believed because they had met Jesus for themselves (John 4:1-42).

This story points to the importance of sharing our own faith story. There are other persons listening who may be encouraged to meet the living Christ through our story of faith. In the end, they too may experience the living Christ in their own lives. Stories can and do empower and transform.

> *Myth-Conception:* The goal of evangelism is to get someone to "sign on the dotted line." That is the end of evangelism. It is enough if we just do everything we can to get persons to say "yes." Having persons "make a decision for Christ" is ultimate. Our job is to get someone to make the decision for Christ.

When we experience the living Christ in our own lives, we discover how God can transform and empower us to be the people we were created to be. Our response to God's grace is a desire to reach out to others. It is painful to see persons agonizing over the meaning of life. In our desire to reach out to others, however, we need to remember the meaning of new wine and the basic goal of relational evangelism, which is to enter into a deep and lasting relationship with Jesus Christ.

The "method" of evangelism is important. Studies show that when people are called to make a commitment through manipulation and pressure, they often make a positive commitment. While a great percentage may respond with a "yes," however, they are inactive within six months. On the other hand, more than 90 percent of the people who come to faith because of a relationship with another person remain faithful in their journey. Where relational evangelism and the new wine of Jesus' Spirit are concerned, just any kind of commitment will not do.

If we look carefully at the biblical story, we see that it was not enough that persons followed Jesus. Paul was continually writing letters to the churches and to young Christians to help them grow in the faith. From early church history we know that there were systems of education established to help people learn about the faith, experience the living Christ, and grow in their faith.

"Yes" is not the end. It is, in a sense, only the beginning of a journey that will last, we hope, for a lifetime. Richard Osmer says,

> An important part of ministry with youth is helping them develop a deeper and more personal relationship with God. Intentional instruction and individual guidance in the historic disciplines of personal prayer, corporate worship, and Christian service are essential to support growth in this relationship."[2]

Entering into a relationship with Jesus Christ, and receiving the new wine of his Spirit, calls for ongoing relationships, ministry groups, and new habits of living. New wine encourages us both corporately and individually to grow in our relationship with God, others, and the world. (For more information on discipleship groups for youth, see *Branch Groups*, available from Discipleship Resources, order no. DR067B.)

Myth-Conception: When we evangelize, we are responsible for the outcome. Since we are the ones who witness and invite, we can take the credit if someone accepts our witness. Likewise, we bear the responsibility if persons reject our witness.

Evangelization, according to George Morris, is "spreading the gospel of the kingdom of God by word and deed and then waiting in respectful humility and working with expectant hope."[3] Evangelism is the sharing of the good news of Jesus Christ. Our role is to be faithful and obedient to the nudgings and proddings of God's Spirit in reaching out to persons around us.

In this regard, we need to remember Jesus' parable of the growing seed (Mark 4:26-29). We do not know how God causes a planted seed to grow. Our job is simply to be faithful in planting. God brings about the growth. God is active in the lives of persons at all times—before we are present with them, as we are present with them, and after we leave.

God's grace is offered to persons in a variety of ways. It is God's Spirit that transforms. Our responsibility is not to change people. Our responsibility is to be faithful disciples and witnesses—responding to the call of God in our lives in every situation.

> *Myth-Conception:* Everyone who is invited to meet the living Christ will respond positively. Therefore, if someone has not said "yes," it is because the good news has not been offered properly.

We can make mistakes in the way we share the gospel. This is true. But even when we share very effectively, people will not always respond positively. God has given people the capacity to resist grace. Jesus confronted the rich young ruler with the radical nature of the gospel for his life. According to the account we have received, the young man's response was not positive (Mark 10:17-22).

In the parable of the prodigal son, one son is welcomed back into the household, not as servant but as son. The second son is also invited into the party. But the parable ends with the second son still standing outside pouting and angry about what to him seemed the unfair favoritism shown to his brother (Luke 15:11-32).

People have had different life experiences. Some need more time to recognize and affirm a relationship with God. Some come seeking and expecting, like the woman in the crowd who reached to touch the hem of Jesus' robe (Matthew 9:20-22). Some come seeking, but like Zacchaeus they feel they must remain on the fringes (Luke 19:2-9). Jesus reaches out to all of them to welcome them.

Saul, present at the stoning of Stephen, could hardly have been unaffected by the witness of this Christian. And, while Saul was in the presence of faithful Christians, God was acting in his life. Yet, it was not until his experience on the Damascus Road that Saul became Paul (Acts 9:1-9). Some people will receive the gospel immediately. Some will struggle and receive Christ only at a point in the future. And some, according to the mystery of God's grace will not receive the gospel at all. God has so created us that, in grace, we can yet resist and reject grace. This is why evangelism itself has to be *relational*. Creating new wineskins for ministry in this connection means helping youth find ways to share faith which leave them open to accept people even when the people reject the witness.

> *Myth-Conception:* Growth in faith can take place in isolation, apart from other people.

Growth does not take place in a vacuum. For Christians, and particularly for persons in the Wesleyan tradition, community is a vital part of our spiritual growth and journey. The early church witnessed and served in the world and then gathered again and again for prayer, for support, and for worship. In the eighteenth century, as people expressed a desire for faith, Wesley immediately gathered them into groups that they might grow and become accountable to each other in their journey. We learn from one another; we encourage one another; we pray for one another. As Christians, we are a part of the Body of Christ. We need to regularly participate in the community of faith. "Spiritual formation simply is not intelligible apart from the communal context and faith tradition in which people are formed."[4]

> *Myth-Conception:* We must "target" the leaders. We must primarily focus on the youth who are leaders so others will follow the decisions they make.

Jesus did go to leaders. He went to those who had an established fishing business. He also talked with the rich young ruler. One of Paul's companions in the early church was a physician. In many areas of the world where people live in a tribal culture, the leader of the tribe has power over the beliefs and the practices of the tribe. In these settings missionaries from around the world have approached the tribal leader first.

The radical nature of the gospel, however, is that Jesus valued all people. Jesus related to people beyond the cultural norms of the day. The norm of the day was that a person from Galilee would not speak to a person from Samaria. A man was not to address a woman in public. Yet, Jesus sat at the well and spoke to a Samaritan woman about her life and need for living water (John 4:4-9). The religious practices of the day forbade contact with those who had leprosy and demanded ritual cleansing after touching those who were "unclean." Jesus went to a man who was a leper and touched him and healed him (Matthew 8:1-3). The people around Jesus were trying to protect him from those who were "not important." Jesus invited and welcomed the children. He made time for them (Mark 10:13-16).

The New Testament is filled with stories and parables that declare the importance of those who are poor, powerless, and outcast in society. The new wine of the Spirit calls us to the same set of values in our day. In some respects, it is important to reach out to leaders who can have an influence on other persons. Yet, in the history and tradition of the Christian faith, reaching out to the powerless, downtrodden, and dispossessed is an even more basic priority. This is an extremely important issue for youth who, as much as anyone, are concerned about their place in "the group."

Consider, for example, the case of Daniel. Daniel was a dropout from school, but felt welcomed in the youth group. He was invited by a friend. His initial feelings of being welcomed by the group were dashed, however, when he found that he was not really accepted in the ongoing activities and relationships of the group. He was an outsider. Eventually he dropped out.

Or, consider Tammy. Tammy's family had been an active part of the congregation for a long time. Tammy was encouraged to attend, and she wanted to be a part of the youth group. She was bold to share her ideas and wanted to be in leadership. Soon, however, she found that the others always left her to herself. Or, worse yet, they sometimes played jokes on her to make her feel unimportant or dumb. While she remained a part of the youth group, her attendance became sporadic, and her self-esteem suffered. She did not experience God's love for her through the group.

Another situation is that of Todd. Todd was from a poor family. He lived in a trailer. He was the only one in the youth group from that setting. Todd wanted to be good friends with the key leader in the group, but he did not have the social skills necessary to make that happen. He deeply felt the hurt of being an outsider and, eventually, he stopped coming to the youth group. Todd died when he was a senior in high school. He told one older adult in the congregation about his feelings of not being liked by the group, but he could not tell the group or the youth leader. The group members realized what they had done and felt great hurt at the way they had treated Todd, but it was too late.

Finally, consider the very different story of Jennifer. Jennifer was sexually abused by her stepfather. She withdrew and felt she was not worth anything as a human being. She felt her problems must be her fault. She was ashamed. She did not feel that she could tell anyone. Even though they did not know the underlying problem, the youth group and leader continued to encourage Jennifer and to affirm her gifts. She finally found courage to tell her mother. As a result of the care she received in the youth group, Jennifer found healing in Christ.

We have looked in this chapter at a great many false ideas about the nature of evangelism in youth ministry. The guiding thought in all that we have shared has been Jesus' image of new wine—that is, the vision of a new relationship with God in Christ by the Spirit— and the need for new wineskins, new forms of ministry that allow this relationship to blossom and flourish. As adults who work in various forms of youth ministry, the promise of new wine—of healing and new life in Christ—calls us to find new ways of reaching out to those on the edges. Our own relationship with Christ compels us to extend *his* hospitality to those youth who are not in the center of popularity, those who are not on the inside of their peer groups. In this way, our lives can model the essence of relational evangelism, which means we welcome the stranger and reach out in authentic ways to the powerless and abused. Christ calls us to this lifestyle!

CHAPTER 6
NEW WINESKINS:
FERMENTING AND GROWING

I n order to celebrate the new wine of life in Jesus Christ, persons involved with ministries of evangelism must be able to build *relationships* with contemporary youth. But how do you move from old wineskins to new ones?

Thus far we have looked at the meaning of new wine and new wineskins in the Bible. We have described some of the features of youth culture in the '90s. And we have given an account of a number of old wineskins—old ideas about youth, adults, and ways of approaching ministries of evangelism. Our objective now is to move beyond these foundations and to begin to think about forms of ministry, new wineskins, that promise to enhance relational evangelism in the '90s, and thus to share the new wine of life in Christ.

To this end, we want to describe some models of existing ministries that have, in our estimation, made way for the new wine. These models show how new ministries with youth have taken shape in other settings. They cannot replace the need to plan ministry in response to your own unique setting, in contact with the specific needs of young people in your community. But they may suggest some possibilities that stimulate your own visioning process.

The youth and adults who planned these models were tuned into the real needs of youth in their communities. They took time to understand who youth are—psychologically, emotionally, spiritually, and physically. They understood that youth are always changing, always searching, always growing. They knew that, if they wanted to lay the foundations for vital ministries of evangelism with youth, they had to start by knowing and accepting who youth are. Therefore, we commend their example to you.

As you think about how to proceed, don't be afraid to be creative in your own local situation. Allow God's Spirit to direct you, and the youth with whom you work, to discover who teens are in your area. Pay attention to who the youth are—both within your existing congregation and beyond in the surrounding community. Spend time with your youth council, talking about real needs and praying for visions of new forms of youth ministry and evangelism. Plan a retreat with adults and youth to consider how to incorporate and to affirm evangelism in every facet of youth programming. Write some specific goals and objectives for intentional evangelistic outreach. And use the models in this chapter to stimulate your own visioning process.

Variety of Programming

Let's set the scene. It is planning time for the Council on Ministries. Last year two new classes were added to the Sunday school program for adults to meet the varying interests of adults. A new Bible study group and a group to start new ministries of caring were added during the week. The Council on Ministries understood that it was important to provide a variety of programs and ministries for adults in order to help them in their spiritual growth.

When planning takes place for youth programming and ministries in your church, who is it that provides a variety of options and ministries for and with youth? In many cases it is the youth council. Whoever does it, someone needs to remind the planning team that youth, like adults, are not all alike.

Tuwanda comes from a home where family devotions and conversations about the faith are common. She wants a group experience that will challenge her in her faith journey, help her grow in faith, and encourage her to apply her faith commitments to decisions about life.

John's family has not been part of the church. He's not sure that it is important to be in church. However, he enjoys being with his friend David, so he goes to the evening youth group at church. He does not particularly want to spend a lot of time talking about the Bible or praying.

The life histories and experiences of these young people are different. The good news of Christ can enable each of them to become the persons they were created to be and to fully live life. Yet, their immediate needs vary. Tuwanda wishes to spend considerable time talking about how faith relates to the decisions she is facing, what the scriptures say to her life today. John is somewhat curious about the stories in the Bible, but he is not ready to spend a lot of time exploring the scriptures in depth.

Making way for the new wine of relationship with Jesus Christ means providing a variety of settings where each person can explore the Christian faith for his or her life. Youth ministry in the '90s must recognize and affirm the need in each congregation to provide *options* for youth. Not every teen will be at every activity. Think of the youth in your church and community. How do their needs vary and how can a variety of ministries be provided to reach out to them?

Think of the programs that are often included in youth ministry: confirmation, workcamps, Sunday school, and Sunday evening programs. In addition to these, one church reported that programs for the youth included regular Tuesday evening discussions, a 6:30 A.M. Bible study, peer counseling, a newsletter, and classes for parents. Harry and Mabel raised the question at Administrative Council, "Why aren't all the youth at all the programs? There are only six teens at Tuesday night discussion and three at Bible study." The youth coordinator explained: "In this decade we cannot judge the effectiveness of youth ministry by the percentage of teens involved in each option. These programs were developed to meet specific needs."

Welcoming Newcomers and Persons Who Return

Kim and her family had just arrived in their new town. As Kim walked to her Sunday school class, she was scared. She didn't know anyone. She had to fight back tears. She missed her friends and was very lonely. Her fears disappeared when she was met at the door by Renee. Renee spoke to Kim in a reassuring way and welcomed her to the class. As Renee introduced Kim to new friends, Renee talked of her own fear when she moved to the community just two years ago. The teacher made a special point of explaining what the class was doing. Kim was surprised when, in the middle of the week, she received a note from the teacher and a phone call from Renee.

Hospitality is one of the keys to the spirit of relational evangelism in every generation. Providing an atmosphere where teens feel welcome is a reflection on our belief that God is a loving God. There are several ways to extend hospitality to the stranger.

1. Occasionally have programs for youth where they are reminded what it feels like to be new. One way to do this is through role plays.

2. Designate one or more youth to serve as the "welcoming committee." This task can be rotated monthly. The job is to greet new teens at the door, introduce them to everyone in the class, and sit with them. A "welcomer" should also make sure newcomers are included in discussions. Ask for the newcomer's name, address, phone number, and school. A phone call and/or visit with the newcomer during the week provides a warm welcome. During the visit, invite the newcomer to other youth activities, and be prepared to answer questions about the church and youth programs.

3. The teacher, advisor, or group leader also needs to take initiative. Make sure the newcomer is included in the discussion. Make contact with the teen during the week. If the person does not return the next week, make contact to let the teen know he or she was missed.

In addition, consider the following tips to make your follow-up contacts more effective. Any contact or recontact needs to be done with care so that the call is perceived as a caring call and not a "pushy sales pitch." Since youth are often still under adult care, it may help to make contact with the parent or adult caregiver. Welcome the opportunity to provide information about youth ministry in your congregation. A good way to discover some of the strengths of your youth ministry is simply to ask new youth why they decided to stay. Finally, if you find that you have visitors who do not return, you may want to honestly look at your "hospitality meter." How inviting and open is your youth ministry? Call some of those who did not return and ask what it was that made them decide not to return. If we want to help teens relate to God as friends, we need to be friends!

Along with welcoming newcomers, it is also important to stay in touch with those who were active for awhile and then dropped out. Consider the case of Deana. . . . Deana came to Sunday school for a while, but she was upset one day at the way some of the others in the class treated her. She did not come back for two months. Then, her relationships in school changed, and she felt that the Sunday school class might again provide some of the community she needed. She wondered if the class would welcome her back or if they would reject her for being away.

Teens, like adults, leave groups for all kinds of reasons. They may have had a lot of school work in addition to a heavy work schedule or additional responsibilities at home. They may have felt pushed to the point where they had to give up something. So they dropped the activities at church. It could be they were no longer a part of any group. They may have had an argument with another person in the group and left with hard feelings. It could be there was just a misunderstanding. Whatever the reasons, whenever a teen leaves a group it is important that caring contact be maintained.

The following suggestions may be helpful as you consider ways to renew relationship with those who have dropped away.

1. A conversation or contact may help correct a misunderstanding.
2. A visit or note lets the teen know you and others do think he or she is important.
3. The church is a place where we stand at the door again and again to invite and to welcome persons back into the community of faith.

The ways in which we do or do not reach out to youth are directly connected with the ways they experience or fail to experience God's seeking love and grace in their lives. In the midst of feeling unlovable, a contact from another teen or an adult leader can help a young person experience God's love in a personal way. If we talk about God's inclusive and forgiving love, our actions need to show that love.

When a youth does come back, the adult leader should take primary responsibility for creating and ensuring experiences of genuine hospitality. In the mode of peer counseling, a group of teens can also be trained to welcome those who are returning. Welcoming the returning youth may not feel "natural" for some teens, however. Therefore, since people have different needs and personalities, it may sometimes be helpful to select a particular teen who can relate to the specific youth who is returning. In any case, the adult worker has a special role to encourage everyone to reach out to those who are returning to the group.

Clubs, Meetings, and Study Groups That Help Youth Develop Their Spiritual Life

Many youth are gathering to meet in small groups to strengthen their spiritual development. Group life and experience is, indeed, one of the most natural ways to catch the vision of relational evangelism. While these groups can take many different forms, one very effective model is the "Breakfast Club." The Breakfast Club is a group of youth who meet before school. The youth usually meet at someone's home. They have breakfast, Bible study, and prayer.

Breakfast Clubs were started, in part, because of the busy schedule of contemporary youth. When the idea was first suggested, some people argued that youth were too busy to meet for Bible study. Others objected that young people would never get up early to meet for Bible study. Against the odds, several congregations tried Breakfast Clubs. Some congregations organized them during Lent. The assumption was that the group would only be a Lenten study. The youth, however, wanted to continue after Lent.

The exciting thing about Breakfast Clubs is that youth who want to study the Bible are willing to forego sleep one morning a week. By meeting in the early morning, it frees them after school and in the evening for homework, part-time jobs, and other activities.

Another model for small group life is that of "Branch Groups." Branch Groups are an adaptation of John Wesley's class meetings. Branch Groups are being formed in many congregations, especially those that have experienced Covenant Discipleship groups.

A Branch Group is comprised of a small group of youth who meet once a week with an adult leader. The meetings center around a covenant that group members have agreed upon. The covenant contains goals that help youth in their spiritual growth.

Branch Groups are making a difference in the lives of youth. Julie Overton, a member of a Branch Group at Union United Methodist Church, Belleville, Illinois, writes: "The covenant has given me a chance to evaluate my weaknesses and my strengths. I've found that my weaknesses generally have to do with studying the Bible and my strengths come from dealing with people. The Branch Group is a

place to share our lives in relation to God. The community service
I've done in the past year has been the most rewarding. I had never
been involved in anything before joining the Branch Group. Now I
am doing volunteer work at the Women's Crisis Center."[1] A handbook called *Branch Groups* (order no. DR067B) can be ordered
from Discipleship Resources, P. O. Box 189, Nashville, Tennessee
37202, 615-340-7284.

Another model is the Chrysalis event. Chrysalis is a three-day
spiritual retreat, an adaptation of the Walk to Emmaus. Chrysalis is
open to high school sophomores, juniors, and seniors who want to
strengthen their friendship with Christ. It is for teens who have
unanswered questions about prayer, study, and sharing their faith,
and who understand that being a friend of Christ carries responsibilities. (For more information on the Chrysalis, write to National
Chrysalis Director, The Upper Room, P. O. Box 189, Nashville, TN
37202.)

"Bible and Bologna" is an endeavor started by Bethel United
Methodist Church in Wichita, Kansas. The church, located across
the street from a city high school, started a lunchtime program.
Students bring their lunch (often bologna sandwiches) and have a
short Bible study. The time they spend at the church is only as long
as their lunch period. This outreach provides a way for youth to
meet and eat together as well as to study the Bible.

Park Avenue United Methodist Church in Minneapolis, Min-
nesota, has several outreach programs to youth in their community.
One of the most exciting programs is their sports program which
sponsors several different sports activities for the youth of the community. To recruit youth for the teams, the adults visit the schools
and eat lunch with the students. This provides a way for the youth
counselors to meet the youth in their own setting. The conversation is very informal and often focuses on the sports program
itself, rather than on religious topics.

A significant part of the ongoing sports program of Park Avenue,
nevertheless, is that the program is Christ-centered. Though the
adults do not launch the program with a religious discussion, they
are very willing to share their faith and beliefs with the youth. The
sports program has often been a way to introduce youth into other
programs and ministries the church has to offer.

Heritage Hills Youth Club in Pulaski, Pennsylvania, presents another model. Heritage Hills is a mission outpost project of a neighboring United Methodist church. The youth club is in a trailer court and ministers to youth and young adults.

The mission endeavor began when one woman realized that she was the only one who left the rural trailer court on Sunday morning for worship. With the help of her congregation and money from the Youth Service Fund, the church bought a trailer and began to have Sunday school.

The youth of the trailer park, not having a place to gather, became part of the ministry. They raised funds and built on a room to the original trailer. They have a place where the message about Jesus Christ is told in a way they can understand. The youth now have a safe place where they can address some of their own problems in a caring environment, and they are growing in relationship with Jesus Christ.

At-Risk Youth

A number of congregations across the nation have recognized the opportunity for building relationships with at-risk youth. Echo Park United Methodist Church in Los Angeles, California, is one example. Echo Park is a culturally diverse, inner-city congregation. Ten years ago the congregation was all Anglo American. Now, the community is transitional with the majority of persons being refugees from Sri Lanka and the countries of Central and South America. The majority of the constituents of Echo Park Church are below the age of eighteen.

The youth have to contend with a host of problems including gangs, violence, and drugs. To combat these devastating problems, and to incorporate the youth into the congregation, the church runs a number of programs ranging from tutoring to theater, music, and other cultural arts programs. The youth regularly share their music and drama in church. This congregation takes seriously the call to share the new wine of relationship in Jesus Christ with the youth in the community. In turn the youth are turned on to the gospel and to the church.

A congregation in Tampa, Florida, provides another example. This congregation has a program for the teens from the community who are in eighth and ninth grades. The program is held on Friday nights and includes dancing, food, and music. The style of the program is intentionally designed to appeal to youth culture. This church provides a safe place for youth to gather. As in most congregations with effective ministries with youth, there are many adults available for interaction and discussion.

Consider also the model of Ben Hill Church in Atlanta, Georgia. This vital congregation has adopted the Kimberly Court Housing Project. The church is reaching out to share a loving and caring ministry with the youth and children of the area.[2]

St. Paul and Calvary East Churches of Louisville, Kentucky, have found a special ministry. They cooperate with the Youth Offender Rehabilitation Program in a ministry for young first-time offenders. The teens in this program often feel they have been left alone to face life's problems. Workers in the program form relationships with the teens and help them see that they are not alone. The offenders are directed to make restitution to their victims and encouraged to form new patterns and directions for life. In the relationships that are formed, teens are able to see forgiveness and new hope as people share God's forgiveness and love in Christ with them.

A final model of ministry with youth at risk is that of "The Shared Ministry," an ecumenical, inner-city parish in Harrisburg, Pennsylvania. Several years ago, because of prayer and a concern for the community youth who attended church, a school incentive program was started. The first year youth were rewarded for not missing school more than three days per semester. Such rewards included dinners at restaurants, trips to pro football and hockey games, and a trip to Philadelphia. Incentives are important in the lives of teens who are from situations where they see little hope. The second year the school incentive program not only focused on attendance, but also on grades. To help youth strive for better grades, a tutoring program was started. The success of the program was shown when three previously failing teens graduated from high school. Two of them went on to college and one has earned a master's degree. These teens saw hope because people made the hope of Christ tangible. They were able to experience themselves as valued people of God.

Mentoring

Another form of ministry with real potential for building relationships with youth in the '90s is mentoring. Rural Mission, Inc. is a cooperative ministry on Johns Island, South Carolina. The ministry was started to ensure that youth could discover their own spiritual and cultural history. The youth were asked to interview and to record the life experiences of the grandparents of the community by asking why Jesus Christ was important to them.

The outcome was twofold. The most tangible outcome was that the youth produced a resource that recounted the spiritual history of their people in the islands. The other outcome, just as significant in its own way, was that the youth established significant relationships with the older adults. By sharing their faith stories, the adults had a significant impact on the faith journeys of the young people.

There are many ways to establish mentoring relationships. Shelly is an eleventh grader serving on the finance committee in her local church. By working with this committee and helping to make decisions about her congregation's finances, Shelly's own faith has been stretched, expanded, and deepened.

Bill is an eighth grader who serves on his congregation's committee on outreach. Once a month he volunteers with the local mission feeding program. Along with other members of the congregation, Bill serves meals to about 120 men, women, and children who eat at the mission.

Shelly and Bill became involved in the committees of their local church because of one adult—Betty. Betty volunteered to help the youth of her congregation find ways to serve on boards and committees. She believed the youth could make valuable contributions to committees. And she foresaw that the young people would be nurtured in their faith as well.

At the beginning of each year, Betty meets with all youth who have been selected to serve on the board and committees. She provides each young person with a description of the function of the assigned committee, as well as detailed outlines of what each committee accomplished the year before. She also cuts out the picture of every committee member from the church's pictorial directory and places each picture on a page with a short biographical sketch.

Betty also talks with the young people after each committee meeting. She asks how the young people felt about the meeting. Did they understand what was going on? How were they treated? Sometimes Betty discovers that she needs to talk with the chairperson of a particular committee about intentionally including the youth in the discussions.

Betty has become an important adult in the lives of the young people with whom she works. She is someone they can turn to with questions and concerns. She is open to talking with them about their role in the life of the congregation. Betty also encourages them to ask questions about their faith. She tries to get them to think about how their beliefs interact with the decisions the committees make.

Another model of mentoring is that of Second United Methodist Church. Second Church cares about its youth. The church has devised several ways to let the youth know they are loved. During midterms and final exams, each young person gets a telephone call every morning. The call is simply to let the youth know that people are praying for them during the exams.

Second Church also makes sure that at least one adult attends every event where one of the youth is involved. This includes all sports events, school plays, recitals, etc. The adult's role is to make personal contact with the young person after the event. The main objective is to give tangible proof of support, to show the young people that their congregation really does care. As a result, there is no doubt in the minds of these youth that they are special.

Congregations with effective youth ministries often emphasize ministries of *families* with youth. The Search Institute study found that teenagers have a more integrated faith when they have been able to talk about faith issues with their fathers or other relatives. The study also reported that, for 56 percent of United Methodist teens, and for 57 percent of the adults in The United Methodist Church, this has rarely or never happened.[3] This statistic would suggest that an effective ministry with youth in the church must necessarily include a ministry with the parents of the teens.

Some churches have formed support groups for parents of teens. These groups bring parents together occasionally to talk about such issues as curfew, friends, being a single parent of a teenager, and rules. Such groups offer a real sense of support and encouragement to the parents involved.

One congregation organized a Sunday school class for parents of teenagers. The focus of the class was to help parents explore their own faith in light of living with a teenager. As a result, the parents also discovered ways to talk about their faith with their teens.

The mobility of contemporary society suggests another reason why mentoring can be so important. For many teens, there are few if any adult relatives—apart from their parents—with whom they can form close, caring relationships. Therefore, some churches, like Castleton United Methodist Church in Indianapolis, Indiana, have set high goals for training adults to be in ministry with youth. Currently, Castleton has trained one adult for every six teens in their ministry program. The goal is one adult for every three youth involved.[4]

Adults who train to be in ministry with youth are not chaperones or patrol guards. They are people who can relate to teens as genuine friends in and with Christ.

Sharing Faith

Relational evangelism and "verbal" evangelism are sometimes set in contrast. They don't have to be. In keeping with our initial definition, relational evangelism is "inviting" people into relationship with Jesus Christ. One model that combines these dimensions very effectively is the Youth Lay Witness Mission. In order to plan YLWM, a congregation requests a coordinator for a weekend experience, Friday through Sunday morning. A visiting team of youth comes from various churches to share fellowship together, to witness to their faith in Jesus Christ, and to encourage the teens in the host congregation to share their own experiences with Christ. Often new and renewed commitments are made during the weekend.

One teen shared at the close of a weekend that she was now able to be more open with her mother. She had a sense of release from feelings of anger toward her. Likewise, two young men felt they could be more supportive and encouraging of one another as they tried to live out their Christian faith in the school setting. And some other young people decided to begin a Bible study at school. More information on the Youth Lay Witness Mission may be obtained from: Lay Witness Mission, General Board of Discipleship, P. O. Box 840, Nashville, TN 37202.

Some other models that strengthen the relationship between relational and verbal evangelism are "Have I Got News for You," and the lay speaking program of the General Board of Discipleship.

"Have I Got News for You" is a study for teens in how to share their faith with other teens. Available from Cokesbury bookstores, it includes a Leader's Guide and a book for teen participants.

Traditionally, lay speaking schools have been thought of as being for adults only. However, several youth have broken that barrier and become certified lay speakers. Deborah and Mary Anne are two such youth. These two young women finished both the introductory and the advanced lay speaking courses. As certified lay speakers, they have preached several sermons in churches around Las Vegas. Deborah and Mary Anne also spoke at the youth service of their annual conference. Through study and sermons, they are able to share their faith with others.

Experiences Beyond the Local Church

Technology has brought the world together in a way never before imagined. Today, we experience more exposure to other countries, other cultures, and other ideologies, than ever before. Transportation now allows us to be in another part of our vast country in a matter of hours and across the globe in a day. Television not only reports news but lets us hear conversations in other languages with translation quickly following. Now more than ever we are forced to see the world as a global community. We live in an era when the decisions we make in our own community affect others around the world. Because of this, part of the task of relational evangelism in the '90s must be to help young people experience and share with other Christians and cultures around the globe.

In March 1990, a cluster of churches in New Jersey celebrated a New Life Mission with a pastor from South Africa. The mission began with a rally in which 100 youth experienced a tele-link with South Africa. They sang the South African national anthem and joined in prayer with the leaders from South Africa. They heard the story of people in South Africa who struggle with being Christian in a setting where they are experiencing the dehumanization of apartheid.

In 1988 the General Board of Discipleship sponsored the first United Methodist Youth gathering since the formation of The United Methodist Church in 1968. Almost 4,000 senior high youth from across The United Methodist Church came together in Macomb, Illinois, to celebrate their faith and oneness in Christ. Many teens made a commitment to full-time lay and ordained ministry. Hundreds made new and renewed commitments to Christ. One young woman named Susan said, "We don't get to experience events like this in our church. I feel excited about going back and sharing with my group at home." Sean said he had a new appreciation of the church in Sierra Leone because of his time spent with participants from a church there. Joy met new friends from another part of the country and they continue to be in contact. Brent heard God's Word for his life in a new way in the Bible studies. Tim appreciated learning of the support groups formed in other places for persons with addictive behaviors. He came to see that these kinds of problems affect people everywhere, not just in his town. He also realized in a new way why the church is so concerned about such issues.

In 1990, several jurisdictions sponsored Spiritual Life Rallies. These events, like the one in 1988, affirmed youth as vital members of The United Methodist Church. They also helped youth gain a deeper understanding of God in Jesus Christ.

"Youth '91" was another important event. Sponsored by the General Board of Discipleship, the theme was "In Christ We Are Many, We Are One." Similar global events are proposed for the future. Information can be obtained by writing: Director of Education and Ministries for Senior High Youth, General Board of Discipleship, P. O. Box 840, Nashville, Tennessee 37202.

The International Christian Youth Conference is sponsored by the World Evangelism Committee in cooperation with the World Youth Committee of the World Methodist Council. ICYC takes place every three to four years and is aimed at high school seniors and college-age youth. Conferences have been held in England, the Bahamas, Australia, and Mexico. Participants have come from thirty-eight to forty-five countries at each conference. The Section on Evangelism of the General Board of Discipleship coordinates the participation of youth and young adults from The United Methodist Church.

At one conference a youth from a Western country complained about the food in a small group. A member of that small group responded, "I have been giving thanks for the meals we are having. It is the first time in my life I have had food to eat three times a day!" This was particularly startling for the people who were used to having food in abundance. The issue for them was being selective about what they were willing to eat! A new appreciation grew, not only for what persons had, but for the need to reach out to others who did not have the necessities of life.

Jusuf Roni Paul of Indonesia spoke at one conference. He told of his role in the department of religion of his government. He was given the role of reading the Bible so he could write a book about why it was wrong. In the midst of reading the scriptures, he met the living Christ. He told of the change in his life and his imprisonment for the faith. Those who met him and heard his story could not remain the same persons.

After an experience with Christians from other countries, teens have reported that they see others and the world with new eyes. They also experience their own relationship with Christ in new ways. This, too, is evangelism—people, sharing their faith experiences with each other and, thus, moving deeper in their relationships with Christ.

Being part of a connectional church means that United Methodist youth have many such opportunities. Districts, annual conferences, and jurisdictions sponsor numerous events where youth can interact with others and strengthen their faith and witness.

Youth Serving

Sometimes people worry that youth service projects may become spiritually empty—having no emphasis on prayer, Bible study, and openness to God's Spirit. No doubt this can happen, especially if adult leaders feel called upon to set service and spirituality in contrast. But this does not need to be the case. Indeed, in the Bible itself, there is every reason to believe that service to others is an integral part of growing in relationship with Jesus Christ.

Matthew tells the story of the judgment of the nations. The question is asked,

> Lord, when was it that we saw you hungry and gave you food, or thirsty and gave you something to drink? and when was it that we saw you a stranger and welcomed you, or naked and gave you clothing? And when was it that we saw you sick or in prison and visited you? (Matthew 25:37-39).

Jesus responded that when we serve people with these kinds of needs, we serve him. As adults and youth, we are called to serve others as though we are serving Christ. One of the wonderful mysteries of God's grace is that, in and through such service, when we are open to grace, we find the living Christ ministering to us.

Laura is youth director of a church in Alabama. Every year the youth of that church go on a mission trip. An integral part of the trip is Bible study. Each day youth and adults use the study to help them understand their reasons for being in mission. Far from feeling that Bible study and prayer interfere with service, or vice versa, the youth in Laura's group are discovering God's grace in all things. "Doing good" is not just an attempt to be "nice." It is a way of growing in friendship with Christ and living out of the faith perspective.

A number of excellent mission opportunities are available to youth: Appalachian Service Project, Habitat for Humanity, Youth Servant Teams, and Mountain Top. For more information on these programs contact: Director of Education and Ministries for Senior High Youth, General Board of Discipleship, P. O. Box 840, Nashville, TN 37202. For additional mission and workcamp opportunities contact the General Board of Global Ministries, 475 Riverside Drive, New York, NY 10115.

CHAPTER 7
EPILOGUE

"I never look at the masses as my responsibility.
I look at the individual. I can love only one person at a time. I
can feed only one person at a time. . . .
So you begin. . . . I begin. I picked up one person—
maybe if I didn't pick up that one person I wouldn't have
picked up 42,000.
The whole work is only a drop in the ocean. But if I didn't put
the drop in, the ocean would be one drop less.
Same thing for you . . .
same thing in the church where you go
just begin . . . one, one, one.[1]

Mother Teresa has made an immense difference in the lives of
thousands of people. Her touch, her words, her loving are her faith
made visible.

Adults who work with youth make an immense difference in the
lives of countless youth. Caring, sharing, listening, and speaking
words of encouragement are faith made visible.

Youth ministry is exciting and wonderful. When the task seems
too great, remember you are called to be faithful and obedient. You
are called in ministry to relate to teens one by one so that they may
become friends with Christ.

As you grow in your own relationship with Jesus, may you know
the new wine of his Spirit bringing courage and serenity to your life.
As you discern where young people are today, and the possibilities
for ministry in your congregation, may you know the freedom and
creativity of the Spirit to move beyond the old wineskins. And as
you seek to be open to the new wineskins that Jesus taught about so
long ago, may you know God's rich and tangible blessing in your
ministry with youth.

ENDNOTES

Chapter 1

1. Larry Keefauver, *Friends & Faith* (Loveland, Colorado: Group Publishing Co., 1986), p. 17. Reprinted by permission.
2. Merton P. Strommen, *Five Cries of Youth* (San Francisco: Harper & Row Publishers, 1988), p. 111.

Chapter 3

1. *Effective Christian Education: A National Study of Protestant Congregations—A Report for the United Methodist Church* (Minneapolis, MN: Search Institute, 1990), p. 34.
2. Ibid., p. 33.
3. Eugene C. Roehlkepartain, Ed., *Youth Ministry Resource Book* (Loveland, Colorado: Group Publishing Co., 1988), p. 87. Reprinted by permission.
4. "Children & Teens Today," Volume 10, No. 12, August 1990, ATCOM, Inc. (New York, 1990), p. 3.
5. *Youthworker Update*, Volume IV, Number 10, June 1990, Youth Specialties, El Cajon, California, p. 1.
6. "Children & Teens Today," p. 4.
7. Robert Bezilla, Ed., *The Gallup Study on America's Youth* (Princeton, New Jersey: The George H. Gallup International Institute, 1988), p. 185.
8. *Youth Ministry Resource Book*, p. 133.
9. *Highlights of Official Child Neglect and Abuse Reporting 1986.* (1988) The American Humane Association, Denver, Colorado, p. 10.
10. *Youth Ministry Resource Book*, p. 166.
11. Barry D. Garfinkle, Gabrielle A. Carlson, Elizabeth Weller, *Psychiatric Disorders in Children and Adolescents* (Philadelphia: W. B. Saunders Company, 1990), p. 372.
12. *Five Cries of Youth*, p. 34.
13. Richard Osmer, "Challenges to Youth Ministry in Mainline Churches: Thought Provokers," in *Affirmation*, Volume 2, No. 1, p. 7, Spring 1989. Union Theological Seminary in Virginia. This material is reprinted with permission of Union Theological Seminary in Virginia.
14. Ibid.

77

Chapter 4

1. Search Institute, p. 40.
2. Yushi Nomura, *Desert Wisdom* (Garden City, New York: Doubleday & Company, Inc., 1982), p. 3. Used by permission.
3. Stanley Hauerwas and William H. Willimon, *Resident Aliens* (Nashville, TN: Abingdon Press, 1989), p. 95.
4. Harold Kushner, *Who Needs God?* (New York: Summit Books, 1989), p. 30. Copyright © by Harold S. Kushner.
5. *Five Cries of Youth,* p. 88.
6. Search Institute, p. 41.
7. *UMYF Handbook* (Nashville, TN: Discipleship Resources, 1989), p. 1.
8. *Friends & Faith,* p. 20.

Chapter 5

1. Peter M. Morgan, *Story Weaving* (St. Louis, Missouri: CBP Press, 1986), p. 13. Used by permission of CBP Press.
2. Osmer, p. 15.
3. George E. Morris, *The Mystery and Meaning of Christian Conversion* (Nashville, TN: Discipleship Resources, 1981), pp. 53-57.
4. Susanne Johnson, *Christian Spiritual Formation* (Nashville, TN: Abingdon Press, 1989), p. 19.

Chapter 6

1. Phyllis Tyler Wayman and Tom Salsgiver, "As the Twig Is Bent," *the Interpreter,* January 1991, p. 20.
2. Ralph and Nell Mohney, *Churches of Vision* (Nashville, TN: Discipleship Resources, 1990), p. 34.
3. Search Institute, p. 41.
4. *Churches of Vision,* p. 45.

Chapter 7

1. Taken from *Words to Love by . . .* by Mother Teresa, p. 80. Copyright © 1983 by Ave Maria Press, Notre Dame, IN 46556. All rights reserved. Used by permission of the publisher.

BIBLIOGRAPHY

Affirmation, Volume 2, No. 1, Spring, 1989. Union Theological Seminary in Virginia.

Bezilla, Robert, Ed. *The Gallup Study on America's Youth.* Princeton, New Jersey: The George H. Gallup International Institute. 1988.

"Children & Teens Today," Volume 10, No. 12, August 1990. New York: ATCOM, 1990.

Effective Christian Education: A National Study of Protestant Congregations—A Report for the United Methodist Church. (1990). Minneapolis, MN: Search Institute.

Garfinkle, Barry D., Gabrielle A. Carlson, and Elizabeth Weller. *Psychiatric Disorders in Children and Adolescents.* Philadelphia: W. B. Saunders Company, 1990.

Hauerwas, Stanley and William H. Willimon. *Resident Aliens.* Nashville, Tennessee: Abingdon Press, 1989.

Highlights of Official Child Neglect and Abuse Reporting 1986. (1988). Denver, Colorado: The American Humane Association.

Johnson, Susanne. *Christian Spiritual Formation.* Nashville, Tennessee: Abingdon Press, 1989.

Keefauver, Larry. *Friends & Faith.* Loveland, Colorado: Group Publishing Co., 1986.

Kushner, Harold. *Who Needs God?* New York: Summit Books, 1989.

Mohney, Ralph and Nell. *Churches of Vision.* Nashville, Tennessee: Discipleship Resources, 1990.

Morgan, Peter M. *Story Weaving.* St. Louis, Missouri: CBP Press, 1986.

Morris, George. *The Mystery and Meaning of Christian Conversion.* Nashville, Tennessee: Discipleship Resources, 1981.

Mother Teresa. *Words to Live By.* Notre Dame, Indiana: Ava Maria Press, 1983.

Nomura, Yushi. *Desert Wisdom.* Garden City, New York: Doubleday & Company, Inc., 1982.

Roehlkepartain, Eugene C., Ed. *Youth Ministry Resource Book.* Loveland, Colorado: Group Publishing Co., 1988.

Salsgiver, Thomas L. "Idea Mart" in *the Interpreter,* July-August, 1989. United Methodist Communications.

Strommen, Merton P. *Five Cries of Youth.* San Francisco: Harper & Row Publishers, 1988.

Tyler-Wayman, Phyllis and Thomas L. Salsgiver. "A Twig Is Bent," *the Interpreter,* January 1991. United Methodist Communications.

UMYF Handbook. Nashville, TN: Discipleship Resources, 1989.

"We've a Story to Tell to the Nations" in *The United Methodist Hymnal.* Nashville, TN: The United Methodist Publishing House, 1989.

Youthworker Update, Volume IV, Number 10, June 1990. El Cajon, California: Youth Specialties.